"This has been an amazing journey that DeAnna has been a part of, influencing lives through a deep understanding of what's right with the world. My colleagues have been touched deeply by the application of Strengths Strategies in their performance and relationships. Their lives have been changed forever, and we feel the impact of this transformation in our organization."

—Dr. Shari L. Olson, PhD, President of South Mountain Community College—USA

"This book is a masterpiece. The capacity that DeAnna and the team had to combine in their book a set of unique and powerful tools to integrate heart and mind is breathtaking. The result is an in-depth journey to transforming people, organizations, and the world. Thank you for such a precious gift!"

—Marisa Godoi, Gallup-Certified Coach, CEO of Êxito Gestão de Carreira Consulting—Brazil

"Throughout this invaluable book, the talented authors invite you to explore what your own inspiration is. With the effective application of Strengths Strategies, you're empowered to define and embrace 'that song,' which enables your unique, sustainable Shift Up! Written in a personable, clear, and easy-to-digest way from the very first to last page, this book is one I'd highly recommend to all those who aspire to create thought-provoking insights and high-value shifts towards optimal living across their lives."

—Umar Khan, Senior Executive and Strengths Strategy Coach—England

"The book took me from a good place to an elevated place. My perspective literally shifted up. *Shift Up!* works from the inside out, using stories, parables, and truth to help you become more of who you really are. It not only teaches you how to use your strengths to lift yourself up but also allows you to create a life that lifts the world you bump into. I will never look at a bumper car the same again!"

—Tami Hymas, Author, Keynote Speaker,
Beauty Industry Expert—USA

"In this book, DeAnna and team have managed to put together a success formula in a nutshell. They skillfully redefine concepts, like fulfillment, frustration, interdependence, and ICU acknowledgment, in a way that makes realizing our own untapped potential a style of life. We learn that Shift Up! is a choice we can make."

—Hesham Diab, Executive Partner at Tragency—Egypt

"What if everyone could drastically shift perspectives about who they are and how they live in this world? This book achieves two potentially significant results for its readers: It's both highly inspiring and extremely practical. Combining the power of real, life-inspiring stories that you can relate to with clear, easy-to-follow steps, you're offered the possibility of experiencing a Shift Up! for yourself in a matter of only a couple of hours of reading. Don't wait any longer. Dive right into *Shift Up!* and into your journey of rediscovering yourself, your worth, and the worth of people around you."

—Florence Hardy, SSCC, Gallup-Certified Coach—France

"*Shift Up!* shakes down our 'mind-full' lives to a point of clarity through a step-by-step process that is both practical and inspiring. My problems and challenges were powerless over the beauty and possibilities that I started to see and feel within and around me as I read this book. The stories, skillful words, and powerful questions make this book personal and provide not only instant hope but also concrete strategies that will make you feel courageous and vulnerable enough to make effective choices. It's like a sudden burst of energy that has a time-release effect. This book is a *must* for every human being."

—Kit Malvar Llamas, SSCC, Gallup-Certified Coach, Franklin Covey Philippines Facilitator, Camp Explore, Inc. Founder/ Director—Philippines

"To become a butterfly, a caterpillar needs to wait until the right time has come. But for us as humans to transform into people who have lives of interdependence, happiness, and productivity, I would highly recommend this book. It will accelerate your transformation as it did for me."

—Xander Cladder, MWO, Talent Coach and Organizational Consultant—The Netherlands

"In these times when the world is challenged everyday to remain universally peaceful in the midst of different types of violence and anxieties, *Shift Up!* gives hope. The author walks you through the different stages of how to discover, develop, and become your best you, thereby increasing 'your ability to bring your very best to the world!' This book will transform you as a person and transform the quality of your relationships and your environment. What makes this book and its approach such a must-read is the underlying magical, positive energy the author hands over to the reader right from the beginning. It revolutionizes the way you think about yourself and is all about deep appreciation, respect, unconditional love, and peace. Thank you, DeAnna and your team, for supporting us around the globe and creating an environment where people have the chance to be what they are best at: themselves."

—Britta Eremit, Executive Coach, Author, Speaker—Germany

"Whether you're looking to enhance your personal or professional impact on situations, after reading this book and experiencing its grounded narratives from life, you'll never again suffer from blindness of the Depletion Zone, nor be unaware of the presence and need to consciously align your Strengths Strategies to further unlock your acuity of self and others in order to realize your full potential."

—David Ribott, 100 Best Global Coach Leader 2017 Awardee,
International Coach Federation Board Member
for the United Arab Emirates

DEANNA MURPHY

with Lisa Dawn Gregory and Steve Jeffs

Shift Up!

STRENGTHS STRATEGIES
FOR OPTIMAL LIVING

RIVER GROVE
BOOKS

Published by River Grove Books
Austin, TX
www.rivergrovebooks.com

Distributed by River Grove Books

Design and composition by Greenleaf Book Group
Cover design by Greenleaf Book Group

Publisher's Cataloging-in-Publication Data is available.

Print ISBN: 978-1-63299-166-9

eBook ISBN: 978-1-63299-167-6

First Edition

This book is lovingly dedicated to my first cheerleaders and champions, the two people who opened the door to seeing my strengths and their possibilities, the finest parents anyone could ever hope for, Dallas and Judy Thompson. I only hope to one day become the person they saw in me and believed that I already was.

You are here to enrich the world, and you
impoverish yourself if you forget the errand.

—WOODROW WILSON

Contents

Foreword

One of my favorite quotes of all time is by Antoine de Saint-Exupéry, who stated, "A goal without a plan is just a wish." Although being inspired can point you in a desirable direction, you need a plan or strategy for optimal success. Serendipitously, you will get both inspiration and strategies right here in this book, written by DeAnna Murphy and her team, which can make a world of difference to you and your life.

I first met DeAnna while attending a conference in Minnesota on a cold and wet winter day. DeAnna was the first speaker I had the privilege to enjoy, and I have to say I really didn't want to leave the room once she finished her presentation. If you know me, you might know I am a little fussy about the classes I attend when I go to a conference of any kind. This is because I'm used to *being* the speaker. Since my Olympic silver medal victory in 2014, I have delivered hundreds of keynotes all over the world. One of my favorite topics is the subject of this book: how to increase and sustain optimal performance. Throughout DeAnna's session, I was blown away by her vast experience and knowledge of this topic. She had a goal and a plan in place to help all who crossed her path. She had a special way of pulling everyone in and teaching the audience in a way that I had never experienced previously.

As an Olympic medalist and strategic performance consultant, I firmly believe that if you want to be the best at anything, you need to surround yourself with the best. As the conference ended, I jumped at the chance to meet DeAnna and to learn more about her ideas and knowledge surrounding strengths and optimal performance. I was not surprised to discover that she was a regular on the speaking circuit and had international recognition as an author, coach, and organizational development consultant and was particularly known for her riveting and personalized content creation and delivery.

I also learned that she was a well-known speaker in the Middle East and was a regular at International Coach Federation and SHRM conferences, often delivering the top-rated standout sessions at the conferences where she spoke. As I eventually became acquainted with her, I was not surprised to learn that as the CEO of People Acuity™ (a Strengths Strategy® company), she had led her organization into thirty-three countries in its first five years and that she had worked with Fortune 500 companies, global firms, and organizations, both small and large, in all sectors of society. Not to mention she had trained and certified more than 300 coaches who were actively using the more than forty-five unique tools, skills, Strengths Strategies®, and methodologies that she and her team had created.

I have every confidence that as you read this book, you will be as delighted as I have been by my experience with DeAnna and her team. Sift through the pages. You will feel as though you are sitting with her, having a personal conversation. You will sense that she is aware of what is challenging you in your own life and work, as if her awareness of what you need right now were heightened. And you will feel it, right along with her personal attention to you and her desire to positively affect your life. As strange as that may seem, it's true. DeAnna lives her life with her heart wide open and her eyes scanning all of humanity with compassion and kindness, looking for the best in everyone.

If you will take to heart the Strengths Strategies that you read about in this book and put them into practice, you will be astounded by the results. You will find that you can strengthen every relationship and outcome in your life. These strategies will help you focus on the most useful applications for picking up your PACE™ performance. PACE is an acronym we created to help you identify your Purpose, Aim, Construct, and Everyday Action/Accountability and to achieve the goals you set for yourself. If you like, you can set your PACE to guide your goal-setting and application of the content in the pages ahead. We will also revisit this in the Afterword to help you take your goal-setting to the next level.

I strongly encourage you to read a chapter every day or two and to pause at the end of each to identify how you will integrate what you have learned. DeAnna has a proven plan in place that has helped thousands of people worldwide to reach their goals and achieve optimal performance and success in all aspects of their lives. *Shift Up!* can help you do the same and live the life you've always imagined.

NOELLE PIKUS PACE,
Strategic Performance Consultant and
2014 Olympic Silver Medalist: Skeleton

Acknowledgements

This book has been a labor of love and has been in the works for nearly five years. It has been driven by a feeling of connection to you, the person holding this book in your hands, as strange as that may sound, given that we may not yet know each other. To this end, my first acknowledgement is of you and how thinking so much about you has influenced, shaped, and motivated my growth and this work.

Additionally, this book has been significantly influenced by amazing people just like you who have taken their turn at being the wind beneath my wings when I needed it. First and foremost, I wish to acknowledge the impact of my most amazing, patient husband of over thirty-three years, Tony Murphy, without whom I would never have even dared to begin this journey.

And I would add that close behind him are my first practice students, my children, who ended up teaching me more than I ever gave to them. Matt (and Kayla!), Mandy, and Sean Murphy, you are among my greatest heroes and most cherished friends! Thank you for allowing me to be part of your worlds in such profound ways and for teaching me truths that have changed my entire life forever.

Second, I must add that none of this would have ever come about without Lisa Gregory and Steve Jeffs, who are part of the People Acuity™ thought leader team. They are among my most treasured professional confidantes, and each of them has spent hundreds, if not thousands, of hours learning with me, challenging my thinking, and allowing me to be the beneficiary of their wisdom and insight. I adore them, and their names will forever be carried forward with these ideas. Doug Peck, Elizabeth (Beth) Willoughby, and Norma Gilstrap Smiley were also critical to the early development of many of these philosophies and their practical expression.

Many others have also impacted this work and been part of this mighty movement sweeping the earth, as we have tested, tried, and challenged these ideas together. Shari Olson is foremost among them, as she was the first person to hire me to deliver the ideas you will read about here. She believed in me so long ago, even when I tried to talk her out of it! Okokon Udo, an engineer of souls, prompted me to find more in me than I thought was there at a time when I was unsure and still finding my own voice. Additionally, Anne Grete Mazziota and Pam Solberg-Tapper, my first coaches and dear friends, have spent hours working through many of these ideas and have been important contributors.

Linda Shannon, Brent Israelsen, Wyn Dunford, Kurt Schneiber, Brandon Rowberry, Kevin Asbjornson, Kristen Foster, Brent Barnacle, Jenna Claypool, Nick Greer, and my precious brother and sisters, Randy Thompson and Shauna Davis and Terri Abel, have all been powerful, yet quiet, champions and integral to the coming forth of the ideas, tools, and resources that will unfold here. They, along with the growing army of Strengths Strategy Certified Coaches across the world, have been in a grand learning laboratory with me and have been critical in refining and delivering so many of the concepts you will experience in these pages. I love all these amazing people who are drawn to be part of the work of calling forth the value, capabilities, and untapped potential of others!

I would also be remiss if I did not express gratitude to Paul Allen, from the Gallup Organization, who dared me to think big. And to Diana Ceres, the best editor ever, and all the folks at Greenleaf who made this book possible. Finally, and most important of all, I acknowledge that God, by whatever name you may call Him, cares that His precious children across the globe see their value, capabilities, and potential. His hand is everywhere in the work of revealing it, and I have felt His concern for you, and for me, and His guidance in writing this book.

It is a grand puzzle we are all creating together. Everyone matters in it. All it takes is for us to be willing to look close enough to see the value in each and every soul who is part of our lives and the larger unfolding puzzle we're all part of.

Introduction

Your greatest fulfillment and most outstanding performance have the
same common root—your ability to apply your strengths to make
a difference. Knowing your strengths will never lead to living and
working in optimal ways. But knowing and using effective Strengths
Strategies will!

—DEANNA MURPHY, LISA GREGORY, STEVE JEFFS, PEOPLE ACUITY™
THOUGHT LEADER TEAM

I still remember the unforgettable moment when my life literally changed forever—the moment when I set my feet on a
path that I had only dreamed of and that I never expected to see
become a reality. Let me tell you just a little about it, since this
book has everything to do with what happened.

It was the fall of 2009. The country was experiencing the
worst economic recession since the Great Depression. Early
predictions in 2009 suggested we were only halfway through a
recession that had begun in December of 2007 and was expected
to be the longest and most severe recession since World War II.

It was a depressing time for many people, to say the least. At that time, I lived in Beltrami County, in northern Minnesota. It was one of the poorest counties in the state, which had been hard-hit economically. Yet even this would not interfere with making a difficult, but amazing, choice that has since left its footprints all over the globe.

It was a Friday night, and I loved Friday nights! Not because the workweek was over, but because it was date night with my husband of nearly twenty-five years. We had been through hell and high water together and had somehow survived having a son mauled and nearly killed by a bear, navigating a daughter's severe disability for twenty-two years, and responding to another son's snowboarding accident, which had caused a traumatic brain injury and broken back. Additionally, we had known the difficulty of our own health challenges, as well as our career-altering unemployment and relocation. We'd been through a few things together and a lot of life changes. Although, neither of us would have ever predicted the colossal change that would come to our lives because of what happened that night.

I should also add that, despite our many challenges, we would still have said that our lives were more or less wonderful. At the time, we both had work we loved, and I felt especially blessed to have such an exhilarating career. It was my job to oversee all leadership development training and coaching for the Center for Outreach and Innovation (operated by Minnesota State Colleges and Universities), and I had been working through them to build the Strengths-Based Leadership Institute. As part of my role, I'd also delivered nine different FranklinCovey products and helped to create and launch a globally recognized experiential leadership program. I had also been blessed by my professional development. I had become a Gallup-Certified Strengths Performance Coach and experienced coach and leadership development training through the prestigious Coaches Training Institute (CTI). I was truly having a peak performance experience and loved what I did and the people with whom I worked.

Yet, even though all this was true, I had been feeling a quiet tug at my heart and a burning sense that I needed to leave my present work behind and do something that seemed insanely crazy at the time. We were in the middle of a recession. I had a six-figure salary with a great benefits package and was doing something I truly loved. Yet I kept feeling that I needed to create a business that could serve not just Minnesota and the midwestern United States but also the world. I could see it in my mind and had been thinking a lot about it, but I was afraid to leave the security of my job and step into "bigger," whatever that was. It was easier to dream about the business of "unlocking the strengths of the world" as something far off in the distance.

On that long-ago Friday night, as we escaped our children and nestled into a quiet spot in our favorite restaurant, my husband and I found ourselves doing what we always did as best friends. We were catching each other up on our lives and work and talking about the possibilities of our future. It was then that I first shared this dream and began to describe to my sweetheart, Tony, what I was envisioning and why it felt so important to me. Of course, as I described my idea, I was quick to qualify it as something "out there," maybe five years down the road.

That was when Tony's head snapped up. His eyes locked with mine, and his look was tender and full of belief and trust. In that moment he said to me, "For twenty-five years, you have followed my dreams. I think it's time for me to follow yours. If you want to do this, and you believe it is right, then let's not wait. Let's do it now."

In that moment there was a thud in my heart. I was filled with the feeling of fear as well as a sense of awe and of being overcome by his confidence in what I had thought were just the pipe dreams of my heart. But, in that moment, spoken aloud, it was no longer a dream. With his blessing, the planning began almost immediately, and that was the moment that Strengths Strategy® Inc. was breathed into existence. Tony's love and faith gave it life, and he became the wind beneath my wings that still carries me today. He believed in my dream, and in me, and trusted that it could become a gift to others—so much so that he eventually left his own career to oversee all the company's operations and global expansion.

I must say, though, at that time it was an act of pure faith to step into this. We trusted in our hope and the firm belief that if we simply put our feet on the starting line and began to move that the resources and people we needed would come. And come they did! It was less than a year later when I met Steve Jeffs—a Top 50 Global Leadership Coach and internationally acclaimed organizational psychologist—and became gifted by his wisdom and friendship as he joined our team. And shortly after that, I was introduced to Lisa Gregory, a business executive who had been designing and delivering leadership development content for 80 percent of the Fortune 500 and Global 1000 companies. As she joined us, this became the thought leader team made in heaven! We have loved our research and work together and have not looked back since.

It was an exciting time for all of us! The first three years we saw 20 percent quarter-over-quarter growth, which exceeded every expectation we ever set for ourselves. And with the help of many other great people, we also experienced international growth that took us into thirty-three countries within the first six years of operation. Top-rated consultants and coaches seemed magnetized to become part of our work and movement. We quickly found ourselves catapulted into bringing our experiential, transformational learning tools and resources to people and organizations from small organizations all the way to Fortune 100 companies. It has almost been as though it *were* a dream!

Now, nearly eight years from that night so long ago, Lisa, Steve, and I, supported by many others, work shoulder to shoulder in developing the assessment tools, online and live content, resources, and thought leadership for Strengths Strategy's newest company, People Acuity. This company has taken all the brilliance and strengths practices and methodology we had developed before and evolved them to include the insight from more than 200 of the world's top thought leaders and other supporting concepts that more fully meet the needs of today. Our new company has been focused on helping people to see themselves and others with greater clarity, or acuity. We chose this focus because the way you see yourself and others drives all relationships, results, and performance, which is so important to living an optimal life of fulfillment and joy.

This brings us to the subject of this book, which is all about how Strengths Strategies® can help you experience a Shift Up! from the depleting and draining frustration of simply existing to living in the exhilaration of high energy and performance every day. We here at People Acuity know all about that, as we are living in that Optimal Zone™ ourselves and know the excitement, growth, and possibilities attached to it! We don't just teach these truths and strategies; we also practice and strive to become those truths, integrating them into our very way of being. We hold that focusing on your way of seeing and being will have more power to change behavior and performance than focusing directly on behavior or performance ever will.

This first book is our attempt to share with you some of the most impactful Strengths Strategies we have developed and successfully implemented with thousands of people across the globe. They are truly transformational! The moment you set your hand to learning and applying them, you will find their truth in the evidence of your own life. You will feel the power of enhanced relationships and know the excitement of being fully committed to your work and life. You will know the joy of deeper fulfillment and purpose in your personal life and in your work, and you will watch your performance rise, right along with your ability to intelligently influence others to join you in living more optimally. Instead of coercing or driving others, you will inspire them by your own way of seeing and being different.

Each chapter begins with a true story, many of them from the clients and people we have served over the years. Their names and the details of their stories have been changed to honor their privacy. Nonetheless, the anecdotes you read here are all true. In addition to the great stories you will discover, you will also learn some practical and easily applied Strengths Strategies. These simple strategies are intended to be pragmatic and relatable, and you will see that each one includes a step-by-step application process to guide your development and practice. Finally, each chapter will end with a summary of key points and some suggestions for action. By the way, if you are serious about putting some of these amazing ideas into action, you will be excited to find a clear road map for development in the Afterword, which will include the PACE goal-setting system created by our friend and colleague Noelle Pikus Pace, a 2014 Olympic silver medalist and strategic performance expert.

A word of warning, however, as you begin: If you do decide to go beyond merely reading this book and you start to practice these Strengths Strategies, be prepared for a dramatic Shift Up! in your life. Be prepared to feel the exhilaration of being more of who you were born to be, as you anchor confidently in your strengths and in strengths-based strategies that are sure to help you lift off. You see, you will never grow effectively or efficiently if you are trying to fuel your growth by focusing on your weaknesses. This is one of many reasons Strengths Strategies are so powerful, because they will accelerate your energy, performance, and relationships so rapidly and so effectively that you will find yourself being the best you possible.

We trust that this will be as rewarding for you to read as it has been for us to create. And we look forward to joining you on this journey of learning how to Shift Up! where you will discover how to apply Strengths Strategies for Optimal Living to your own life. Happy reading!

DEANNA MURPHY, LISA GREGORY, AND STEVE JEFFS

October 11, 2017

Shift Up! through People Acuity™

> When all is said and done, one of the greatest tragedies of life is to die with your music still in you. What gift might come to the world if you could offer up that slumbering best part of you while you still have the chance? Whose life could you light on fire? Where could you be the catalyst for creating lasting change?
>
> —LISA GREGORY, MS, CPAC

For my dad, love was spelled F-I-S-H-I-N-G. He didn't know how to say "I love you" very well. Indeed, those words seemed to get stuck somewhere between his heart and his throat. Instead, he would ask, "Do you want to go fishing with me on Saturday?" It was his code, and I knew what he meant.

It's funny, but as a kid I didn't even like fishing all that much; but I thought my dad was the greatest guy in the world, and I loved being with him. Besides, I could never get enough of the Canadian Rockies, the blue skies, the clear mountain lakes, and the time away from the city so I could hear the quiet of my own thoughts. Being the oldest of ten children, it was easy to lose myself. I was in my late-teen years with multiple jobs, boy problems, and college looming, and I was busy with what felt like a stressful, complex life.

We were on our way up to Kananaskis Country for some hiking and fishing, and I had been quiet most of the drive. Suddenly, we found ourselves stopped so a huge herd of bighorn sheep could pass. While we were waiting for the sheep to cross, my dad looked over at me. I could feel his tenderness as he studied my troubled features. "What's on your mind?" he asked.

In those few short minutes, it all came tumbling out. The worries about money, friends, and the boy I had been dating for several months. I shared my feelings of inadequacy about college, my future, and never being good enough to be the person that my heart told me I was born to be. As the words poured out of me, my dad listened quietly and waited for the long line of sheep to finish crossing the road.

As the old green Valiant continued the upward climb, he listened until I ran out of words and then responded in a rather unusual way. He began to tell me about a woman who had been an inspiration to him. She was the daughter of Ezra Taft Benson, the fifteenth Secretary of Agriculture during the Eisenhower years. Barbara was a homecoming queen at Brigham Young University (BYU) and was voted the "Friendliest Girl on Campus." She was popular, beautiful, and accomplished. She also was the envy of every girl at BYU and the target of every eligible bachelor. But she was also resolute about who she was, what her personal standards were, and what her integrity meant. She would not let others write her life script for her or tell her how she felt or thought.

He paused mid-story, and I quietly spoke. "I could be like that too, Dad, if I were a homecoming queen." I probably sounded a bit defensive. But he didn't respond. That was when it began to dawn on me that I had missed the whole point of his story. In that moment, something rare happened. As he took his eyes briefly off the road to meet mine, they were filled with tears. When he spoke, all he said was, "You are more of a homecoming queen than you realize."

That was all he needed to say. In that moment, his words seemed to awaken something in me, something I did not fully understand. But I could feel that he could see me, as if he had peered all the way into my soul. He had seen past my teenage sullenness, my fears and self-doubts, and my weaknesses. He didn't judge any of those things. All he seemed to notice were the goodness and possibilities in me, as though I were as beautiful, confident, courageous, smart, and accomplished as Barbara Benson. Although, to him I don't think it mattered if I ever was. He simply saw the best in me, as if I had already become it, and he was just waiting for me to catch up.

Like a Distant Serenade

What is interesting is that I didn't catch up for about thirty more years. You might say I was just a little slow on the uptake. It was not until he was gone and I had a teenager or two of my own that I could finally begin to see what he had been trying to share that day.

It was as though a soft, distant serenade from my childhood, one I had long forgotten, began to stir within me. At first it was just an unnoticed melody playing quietly in the background. But then, as I started to tune into it and feel its warmth, I noticed that it seemed to bring comfort and inspired me to challenge myself. It was like an old friend who had been away for a long time and had come back into my life. Its presence seemed to calm, uplift, and call me to be the person my father had been trying to tell me that I already was.

More and more, I found myself "humming" its unforgettable and familiar tune until, gradually, a more complete song found its way back into my consciousness. Then I couldn't help myself. I had to put words to the music that seemed to call forth something within me, something deep in my soul—something that seemed to invite me to be better, to be more, and to give the best in me to lift and serve others. For the first time, maybe ever, I was not afraid to try.

The words were simple. They were not artistic, nor did they rhyme, but the meaning of them reverberated deeply in every cell of my body. They went something like this:

You are not your beauty or your strength. You are not your popularity. You are not your accomplishments, your performance, or the scorecard of your life experiences.

You are also not reduced by your weakness. Nor by your mistakes and failures. These things are your gifts as much as your strengths and successes and can be a benefit to you if you do not fear them.

If you will let others complete your weakness with their strengths, they will feel valued, and you will feel more whole. Others will have the quiet fulfillment of knowing that they made a difference, and you will get to learn from them. You will be a gift to those who are gifting you.

But even then, never think that your value is equal to the degree to which you add value to others, no matter how well you do it. Never think that your value is based on how much (or how many) people value you. It is simply immeasurable. Your value just is.

You can increase your ability to add value. But no matter how much good you do, or how many accomplishments or friends you have, it will never make you more valuable. You. Just. Are.

The chance that you could find someone like you, with the same strengths you have (in the same order) is 1 in 476 trillion. You are unique.

You can do and be something that no one else in the world can, particularly as you awaken and seek out your unseen possibilities. Your untapped potential is truly a vast, never-ending frontier that eagerly awaits your bold exploration and discovery.

And then, when you add your sorrows, struggles, setbacks, and life experience to your unique strengths equation, you become a powerhouse for unimaginable good—particularly as you let your pain fuel your passion.

When you choose to give from the depth of your inner knowing, you will live your life on fire. No thing, no person can stop you. And you will create endless ripples across the world, leaving a legacy that flows like a river, bringing life to everything it touches.

You were born to make a difference. The only question is, "What will your difference be?"

* * *

This "song" is clearly not finished, and there are other verses that continue to be written. Whenever my life intersects and harmonizes with others who are boldly singing their own songs, the music within me evolves. I hear new additions to an old tune and new lyrics that grow out of the wisdom and wonder I find in others' brilliance. It is as though the beautiful songs around me become interwoven with mine, and we are like ABBA, creating a wonderful new song to ignite and inspire others.

Your song is inside of you as well. It's there whether you know it and can sing it with confidence or not. The truth is that a song exists in everyone. When I think about mine, I'm pretty sure that I had some inkling of it even in my earliest years. When I was young, I sang a much simpler version of it with reckless abandon and a goofy smile to anyone within earshot. I remember one time my grandmother recorded me singing it and then cheered and clapped when I finished, as though I had just won *American Idol!* But over time, the distant serenade faded, almost as if I had never known it. This might be your story as well.

Life-Experience Cataracts

What I've described here is, more or less, the human story. It seems to happen to almost everyone. It comes in response to life experiences that drown out your inner music and gradually change the way you see virtually everything in your life. The fact is you can't live on this planet without having "life-experience cataracts" develop in response to the challenging situations and relationships you encounter. These "cataracts" impair the way you see yourself and others and inform the way you approach life. They also change how you think others see you, even influencing how you respond to others in challenging situations. Your life-experience cataracts unknowingly prompt you to expect that others will judge you before they have the chance (ironically improving the likelihood that they will). Of course, this further reinforces the negative way you see yourself and others and helps to drown out your own song.

Now, if you were to have actual cataracts developing on your eyes, over time the amount of light recognized by your eyes (as reflected across the entire color spectrum) would gradually begin to decrease. You would go from being able to see red, yellow, orange, green, blue, indigo, and violet to seeing largely the red-orange-yellow part of the spectrum (with some green) as your eyes deteriorated. As light gradually disappeared from your sight, the first color to softly fade would be violet, then indigo, followed by blue and eventually green. Soon, everything would simply look more yellow.

Think about the quality of life you would have if the world were seen only through the spectrum of red-orange-yellow, perhaps with a little chartreuse, and growing fuzzier and darker each day. Your visual acuity could become as poor as 20/800, like my friend Doug experienced before his cataract surgery. If you had no way to correct this problem, you might feel sadness when you sensed a stunning scene from nature waiting to take your breath away. Or when you could no longer clearly see the eyes of a child whom you love, or gaze in delight at a beautiful painting or photograph. Ah, what richness would be lost in the absence of such views and experiences!

It is quite likely you would notice such changes in the quality of your vision over time if you had cataracts developing on your eyes. But it may not be so obvious to notice your song fading into a distant memory as your life-experience cataracts develop. Your Self Acuity™ (your ability to see yourself clearly and accurately) can become so fuzzy that, before you know it, you might feel like you don't know your own heart or your own song. Then when someone else begins to sing his or her song, you may try to join in, maybe even trying to own it as though it were yours. But it never feels quite right, because it is not your song. It never was. You were only meant to harmonize with it, not make it yours.

Do you remember ever feeling this way, even a little? Do you remember what it was like to bump into others whose songs sounded so bold, bright, and attractive that you wanted them to be your own? Do you remember how the comparison affected your confidence or your ability to show up authentically in relationships or accomplish difficult things?

This kind of experience is depleting. It sucks the life right out of you. Your energy was likely drained, and I bet you were wishing that somehow you could be better, perform better, or show up in relationships better—anything to stop the swirl of negativity and make the frustration go away. If so, you were probably spending a lot of time in what is called the Depletion Zone™ (standing in stark contrast to the Optimal Zone™). Figure 1.1 illustrates that the Depletion Zone is a place of low energy and low performance, while the Optimal Zone is the opposite. It is typically a place you love to be, where you experience an abundance of high energy and performance.

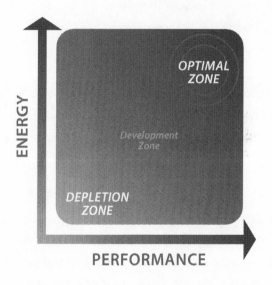

fig. 1.1

When you are in the Depletion Zone, your energy and performance are low, and this is true relative to your tasks and your relationships. It's possible that you have no idea why this is even happening. You may want to blame yourself, feeling like you are not enough—and that is the problem. You can also look outside yourself and wish that something would happen to stop the swirl. It is human to do this and to have no clue how to make it stop. Or you can just go into a self-created silo and push the world away. You might unknowingly try to build walls high enough so you can feel momentarily safe as you begin to block out others' songs. It feels natural to try to tune them out when you don't feel so confident about your own song, let alone trying to harmonize with others.

People Acuity is the ability to clearly see and effectively optimize the value, capabilities, and positive untapped potential in yourself and others.

This is the equivalent of the red-orange-yellow zone where you are stuck seeing through life-experience cataracts that interfere with your view of yourself, others, and the world around you. When you are in the Depletion Zone, the amount of light coming into your view is limited, and you can be sure that your Self Acuity and Other Acuity™ (your ability to see others clearly and accurately) is most likely (and probably unknowingly) fuzzy and quite distorted. Indeed, your People Acuity will be compromised, since you only see part of what is true about yourself and others (Figure 1.2). As you can imagine, this prevents you and others from effectively using the full spectrum of capabilities and potential, since you can't use what you can't see! Just so you have the full definition of People Acuity to accompany Figure 1.2, here it is:

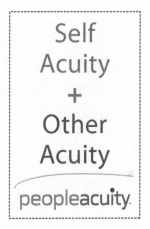

fig. 1.2

If you start to track this a little further, you begin to realize how easily this could cause breakdowns in relationships, teams, and leadership and how projects can run amuck. Or how it might lead to low trust and disengagement (in both work and life), complete with sluggish inaction and feelings of defeat.

19

You may also feel inefficient and unproductive when this happens. Or you can become trapped in frenetic motion (busyness), needing the feeling of being active to drown out the reality that you are feeling stuck. When you don't remember your song or you have stopped believing that you even had one to begin with, the likelihood that you will become stuck in these ways increases. You can even want to run away, quit, or leave, since no one likes being enshrouded in life-sucking energy. All these things are signs that your life-experience cataracts are interfering with your People Acuity.

66

**It's not what happens to you that causes
your feelings, actions, and results.
It's how you choose to see them that does.**

99

Think of it this way: When you have vision problems, you go to an ophthalmologist. Your doctor first must figure out what is ailing you before she can prescribe a solution. However, no eye doctor out there can accurately diagnose your specific life-experience cataracts. When you see that you are repeatedly experiencing the Depletion Zone (and its draining relationships and outcomes), you can be sure you have them, even though you think the problem is caused by something outside of you. While others may be part of what is happening, focusing on them or on things outside of you will not help you see differently. It's not what happens to you that causes your feelings, actions, and results. It's how you choose to see them (Figure 1.3). You can see this in the C2B Different Model shown here, which visually represents the way you can see to be (C2B) different.

fig. 1.3

When your results and relationships and your energy and performance begin to suggest that your People Acuity is suffering, you will benefit from finding your own version of "cataract surgery" to allow more light into your visible spectrum. This will give you more to see with and respond from. This enables you to use the full spectrum of capabilities and untapped potential to change what is happening.

The good news is acquiring People Acuity is not quite as painful as having cataract surgery might be. As soon as you begin to apply Strengths Strategies® (the intentional and strategic use of strengths), you can get out of the Depletion Zone swirl. The idea of Strengths Strategies is important to the People Acuity equation, because your life-experience cataracts can interfere with your ability to see who you are. They leave you feeling small, which will interfere with your willingness to test your capabilities and explore untapped potential. In this book, you will learn the Strengths Strategies to call you back toward your own song. When you are rooted in these strategies, you can find places of success and strength to anchor in and draw confidence from—maybe even enough to help you find your way right out of the Depletion Zone.

Foundational Elements: Looking beneath the Surface

Before you begin to learn the Strengths Strategies that will increase your ability to live more from the Optimal Zone, you'll want to understand where those strategies are focused. Just knowing your strengths is not enough to create the significant Shift Up! you are looking for. You'll want to be strategically directing your strengths so they can target the things that keep you trapped in the Depletion Zone to begin with.

You likely don't realize that beneath your life-sucking Depletion Zone relationships and experiences are three foundational elements that inform the way you see virtually everything in your life. These elements shape the way you engage with others, how you approach situations, and even your own unconscious inner dialogue. Your Self Acuity and Other Acuity are directly affected by these things, as are all your relationships and results in every part of your life. You likely have not known where to look for them before, since they sit below the surface of your conscious thinking most of the time. But as you start to see them, you'll discover why they are so important to your ability to live and work in the Optimal Zone.

Your View of Value

Let's begin by exploring how you might think about your value, where it comes from, how you get it, and how you know you have it. If you are like most people, you are unknowingly trapped in a false view of what makes you or someone else valuable, including the idea that somehow your value fluctuates like the stock market. If you have not met certain unconscious prerequisites, for example, your feeling of value starts to diminish or disappear. This, in turn, will cause you to question your own worth.

Let's look at some of the things most people believe will "earn" value. Check and see if any of these sound like you. You may believe, for example, that your one-way ticket to being of value is to succeed enough, become popular enough, win enough, or make enough money to prove to others that you are worthy. Or you can think that if you work hard enough, do enough, be enough, and have enough, others will like and appreciate you and tell you that you are valuable. If these things happen, then surely you are worthy, right? You might be some-one who needs to have the answers or the information or to know everything to prove your value. Or you may be someone who needs others to like you, trust you, encourage you, or fol-low you as an indication of your worth.

You can find many ways of defining your value from the outside in and not letting it flow from the inside out, as it once did before your life-experience cataracts began to grow. And the truth is that none of these outside-in methods will fill your emptiness in a sustainable way. Almost like an alcoholic needing just one more drink, you may hope for just one more of these things to assure you that you are still okay. That you matter. That you are worthy and valuable. Never mind that continuing to believe this will ultimately suck you right back to the Depletion Zone once the "hit" of your outside-in method wears off.

How You See Strengths and Weaknesses

A close cousin of the way you see value is the way you see strengths and weaknesses and how you evaluate capability. If you're not careful, you can get caught in the need to be seen and appreciated for being strong, so much so that you find yourself scrambling to cover your weaknesses. You can go to great lengths to ensure that others don't discover that you are just as weak as you are strong.

One big problem exists with this line of thinking. You are *both,* because you are a human being. You breathe and have a heartbeat, and this means that you have strengths and weaknesses as part of your makeup. It also means, ironically, that you can make a difference through your strengths *and* your weaknesses. It's the worry about your weaknesses that interferes with your ability to grow your own strengths and to help others effectively grow theirs.

The other interesting thing to know is that if you are not comfortable owning your weaknesses right along with your strengths, you will get caught comparing your capabilities with those of others and feeling as though you're not enough. It is also possible that you look down on others whose capabilities are different from yours and dismiss them because they cannot do what you can. If you are craning your neck up or down based on where you are on the strengths scale, you will surely miss what is right in front of you. You can even lose out on the chance for your weaknesses to improve through the mentorship of others who have different strengths than you, or for you to share your own strengths with someone else.

Discovering and Developing Untapped Potential

Seeing the world through this limiting red-orange-yellow spectrum can leave you almost panicked at the idea of leaving your Comfort Zone and venturing into the unknown and unseen territory of your untapped potential. You are walking in partial darkness and not seeing your own full spectrum of possibilities. That can feel scary. It can be like driving in thick fog, when you can't see beyond its heavy blanket to anticipate or act in ways that keep you and others safe.

For example, if you are asked to do something important

and you have absolutely no idea how to do it, where to start, or what to do, you can get caught in an endless swirl. This can be amplified when you are stuck doing it with others about whom you are uncertain. You may feel like you only want to step forward if you are sure about how people will respond to you, or if you can clearly see where the path is leading and calculate what you will find (before you get there) at every turn and bend. You may want to control the outcomes, plan for every possible failure, and mitigate the likelihood of others judging you when you make mistakes. And this could land you in the Depletion Zone once again.

> 66
>
> ## There is no growth in the Comfort Zone and no comfort in the Growth Zone.
>
> 99

It probably doesn't occur to you that your own self-judgment and your misjudgment of your own endless untapped potential are part of what stops you from accessing it. Your untapped potential is unseen. And if you are like most people, you are just a touch afraid of the unknown. Finding and making use of your untapped potential (and that of others) is always a Growth Zone experience. It is *never* going to be comfortable, so it's best to get over it. According to Professor Noel Tichy, who created this model, you must leave the Comfort Zone to enter the Growth Zone (or Untapped Potential Zone). Figure 1.4 illustrates that there is no growth in the Comfort Zone and no comfort in the Growth Zone.

fig. 1.4

Increasing Your Shift-Up! Ability

The worry and efforts you make to avoid the Panic Zone can be dizzying. This worry can leave you withdrawn, trying to solve it all yourself and cutting yourself off from harmonizing with others who have so much to add. Is it any wonder that you feel stuck sometimes? Is it any wonder that you have Depletion Zone relationships and outcomes more than you would like?

There likely isn't too much comfort in the fact that this

is the natural outcome for you (and every other person on the planet) when life-experience cataracts interfere with your People Acuity. But it doesn't have to stay this way. You can learn how to Shift Up! You can change the way you see and the amount of light you allow into the equation as you apply Strengths Strategies to help you. You can change where you look and access more of the full spectrum of capability and untapped potential both in you and in the richness of others around you. Becoming proficient at using Strengths Strategies empowers you to increase your Shift-Up! Ability, including drawing others out of the Depletion Zone and up (with you) toward the Optimal Zone.

Using Strengths Strategies to change the way you see yourself and others and taking better hold of your inherent value, strengths, weaknesses, and potential, you open a door to a whole new world. When this happens, your energy is consistently higher, right with the quality of your performance in your relationships and activities. This includes something about the way you engage others that energizes them and makes it easier for them to perform well too. You are singing your song and others are harmonizing with you, and the performance is exhilarating! The more you live from the Optimal Zone and gently mentor others around you to join you, the more you experience the optimal performance you long for, along with the remarkable relationships and results that always follow. Over time, this new and better way of seeing and being will replace your tired Depletion Zone habits and life.

When you begin to see yourself differently, it doesn't just

change your Self Acuity. It also starts to influence your Other Acuity, including how you see others and how you think they see you, as shown in Figure 1.5. When you experience this shift, you give yourself and others more grace. You also are more curious and slower to judge. You start to listen longer and deeper, being less attached to getting it right, and are more eager to understand and grow. Eventually, you will find that you have stopped looking up or down at others and instead are standing next to them, looking them straight in the eye without any judgment. Soon, you will notice you can't help but appreciate their value, capabilities, and untapped potential, and you may even yearn to call it forth. You likely won't be able to stop yourself from trying.

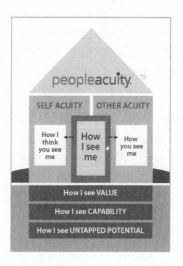

fig. 1.5

Because you can see more, you will be able to access more potential to create new possibilities, results, and relationships. You become a difference-maker, living and operating from the Optimal Zone and bringing others with you. Seeing others and using what you see wisely always leads to higher energy and performance. It can take thirty years for your interaction to work its magic (like it did with me!), but once it happens, there is no going back. When the distant serenade finally finds its way into the soul of a person, the song simply creates a new way of being.

You can be the inspiration to help others Shift Up! as they remember and sing their song again until their music becomes part of the harmony that fills the earth with its grand symphony of possibilities.

It's time for you to sing *your* song—not someone else's. It's exactly what the world is asking for, and you are the only one who knows it. What if your song is the missing melody that could create that new Top 10 hit, one that would prompt the whole world to sing along? What if your song is the answer to a pressing problem the world is facing or something that others around you desperately need in their lives? What if your song helps someone else find hers?

Who knows the Shift Up! that your life can create as you help others see increased light and have access to a more complete spectrum of colors? *Are you ready to Shift Up! through the discovery of some Strengths Strategies?*

If so, read on. And don't be surprised if you start to hum a little as you turn the page.

Growth Zone Challenge: Power Points to See and Shift From

Welcome to the **Growth Zone Challenge**. I invite you to think about where your breakthrough insights have come from and how you will use them to further your growth. Study the list that follows and notice: *Which of the following was your biggest takeaway? What is one thing you will do differently to act on what you have learned? And with whom will you share your learning and commitment?*

- Life-experience cataracts can diminish the spectrum of light that is available to see yourself and others. These cataracts significantly distort your view of who you (and others) really are.

- You know you are experiencing a distorted view because you are stuck in Depletion Zone (low energy and low performance) relationships or experiences, and you don't know how to create a change.

- Three foundational elements underlie your Self and Other Acuity, including the way you see value, capabilities, and untapped potential in yourself and others.

- As your People Acuity sharpens, your Shift-Up! Ability also increases, as does your ability to help others Shift Up!

Shift Up! through Strategic Interdependence™

Strategic Interdependence is always the place of optimal performance! It's also a source of deep fulfillment as you meaningfully contribute to others. You can do so from here with the confidence of knowing that your weaknesses are covered and that they do not negate your value any more than your strengths make you more valuable than others. In the "Us" equation, unimportant pieces do not exist.

—STEVE JEFFS, TOP 50 GLOBAL LEADERSHIP COACH

The world is filled with quiet, unsung heroes who didn't start out with intentional missions of inspiring the world. It's possible they don't even know that others think of them this way. You may even be one of them without realizing it! Whether you are aware of it or not, others around you have undoubtedly experienced a Shift Up! because of you, and maybe in a more profound way than you realize. Your story might never show up on the six o'clock news, but it is written in the hearts of others you have touched.

Let me tell you about someone who is just that kind of man. His story helped me to operate from the Strengths Strategy of choosing Strategic Interdependence at a time in my life when I needed it to escape my own downward spiral. If you haven't heard of Chris Williams before, then his is a name you'll want to remember.

It was late in the evening on a brisk night in February 2007 when Chris and his family were on their way home from a local basketball game. His wife, who was expecting their fifth child, was noticeably tired, but the three children in the backseat were still talking excitedly about the game. As they were heading toward an underpass, Chris was concerned to see a car traveling at a high speed, weaving and bobbing across the middle line toward them. The other driver seemed oblivious to them as he headed straight for their car. Although Chris did his best to maneuver out of the way to avoid a collision, the imposing concrete walls leading into the underpass left him with no recourse except to brace for impact.

Chris's entire life changed in that moment. As he hung upside down from his seatbelt, bleeding and badly wounded, he watched his beautiful wife take her last breath. Their only daughter, Anna, and son Benjamin had also been killed within seconds of the impact. Only he and his son Sam survived the crash, along with his teenage son, Michael, who was not with them at the time. Four precious lives were taken that night by a seventeen-year-old drunk driver—four lives that mattered more than life itself to Chris Williams.

Aloneness, deeper than anything he had ever felt before, overtook him, and Chris became almost instantly engulfed in the darkest sorrow of his life. He found himself wailing and sobbing deeply, almost to the point of drowning out the sirens of the approaching rescue vehicles. In an instant, he had lost almost everything that mattered to him. It felt like his heart had shattered into a million pieces and that nothing could ever put it back together again.

This is where Chris's story begins to take an unusual turn. Before the accident Chris had chosen a simple mantra to guide his thoughts, feelings, and actions. According to a documentary of his story, "Forgiveness: My Burden Was Made Light," released on July 28, 2010, his mantra was to "live as a vessel through which love and light could shine."[1] Every role, every task, and every interaction was driven by his desire to stay in alignment with this. He even went so far as to decide how he would behave whenever it was tested. He made a conscious decision to "fore-give" others before they even hurt him. He wanted to choose grace and kindness, rather than selfishness, resentment, or anger, even when it seemed warranted.

Now, if you are feeling a little surprised by such a notion, then join the club! I remember thinking about this and wondering how remarkable it was to preemptively choose forgiveness, long before it was even needed. I guess it had never occurred to me to "fore-give" anyone. I was also incredulous that he, or

---

1   Chris Williams and Christopher Clark, "Forgiveness: My Burden Was Made Light," filmed 2007 and 2009. The Church of Jesus Christ of Latter-day Saints video, 8:24. Posted July 2010: www.lds.org/media-library/video/2010-07-14-forgiveness-my-burden-was-made-light? category=mormon-messages/mormon-messages-2010&lang=eng.

anyone, could experience such a complete loss without bitterness or anger. He was sorrowful. That was clear. But to choose in advance never to let resentment touch him, particularly in a situation like this? Who could do that? How would you even go about it? At least those were some of the questions swirling in my head as I considered his unique choices.

I have a hard time imagining that Chris ever anticipated that his resolve would be so thoroughly challenged. Yet in his darkest hour and in the middle of the most heart-wrenching situation of his life, he would not be dissuaded from honoring his purpose of reflecting love and light. In ways that can only be described as extraordinary, Chris stayed true to his mantra.

The first inkling of his resolve showed up even as he lay in the emergency room with his neck in a brace and every cell of his body screaming in pain while his youngest son, Sam, was in the next room in critical condition. It was then that he revealed his truest colors as he astonished those attending to him with his first concern being about the driver who was responsible for the tragedy. Through his own tears and pain, he asked about the boy, clearly showing his concern and compassion.

What is ironic to those who might believe that the drunk driver, Cameron White, deserved a taste of the pain is that the driver escaped entirely unharmed. Later, he would feel a completely different kind of pain though, as he pled guilty to four counts of second-degree felony automobile homicide and received a two-and-a-half-year sentence in a correctional facility. By the way, this seemingly "soft" sentence was partly due to Chris, who advocated that he not be tried as an adult. In the days and weeks following the accident, Chris vehemently pled in the media for kindness and grace to be shown to Cameron and expressed a desire for the lightest possible sentence to come to him.

He then went above and beyond what anyone would have expected and began to set up regular visits to mentor and inspire Cameron. He visited Cameron throughout his incarceration, supporting him, encouraging him, and reminding him that his value was separate from his mistakes and did not change because of them. If you are like me, you might be a little curious about what that first visit was like. I've tried to think about it from Cameron's perspective and how he must have felt meeting Chris for the first time. Can you imagine standing across from the man whose family you had killed and looking him in the eye? What would you even say? I'm guessing that Cameron was probably a little frightened. Yet those who are familiar with the story suggest that Cameron's fear was short-lived. He found himself in front of a gentle man who demonstrated nothing but concern for him.

You could even say that Chris's first visit was life-changing for Cameron. Almost the very first words out of Chris's mouth as he reached out his hand with kindness were "I forgive you." Cameron simply wept in disbelief. He kept shaking his head, trying to comprehend how anyone could ever forgive him for what he had done. It was almost more than he knew how to hold, especially as he pictured the faces of Anna, Benjamin, and Chris's wife, Michelle, and thought of the baby Chris would never hold.

During his memorable visits, Chris became bold with Cameron, anticipating the shame Cameron was holding and knowing how destructive it would be to him if he did not release it. Chris extended an invitation, one that would end up affecting thousands of people across the country. He challenged Cameron to pick a date in the future when he would choose to forget what had happened and then turn his pain and experience into a catalyst for helping others.

Cameron was so inspired and encouraged by Chris and his example that he turned his energy in a new direction. He decided that once he was released, he would tour the United States and tell his story with full transparency, educating youth everywhere about underage drinking. And that is exactly what he did.

At this juncture, who knows how many young people have been saved from making choices they would regret? Who knows how many people would not be here had both Cameron and Chris not had the courage to choose Strategic Interdependence when life's circumstances seemed to suck them down? Both men could have suffered lifelong Depletion Zone sentences. Instead, they each chose to Shift Up!

66

Strategic Interdependence is a state or condition characterized by the purposeful use of individual strength for the good of "us" and "others" (not just yourself) and by a willingness to allow weakness to be offset by the strengths of others.

99

Given the importance of the term "Strategic Interdependence" to our discussion in this chapter, I want to offer a working definition for you to think about as we begin our work together: Strategic Interdependence is a state or condition characterized by the wise use of individual strength for the good of "us" and "others" (not just yourself) and by a willingness to allow weakness to be offset by the strengths of others, as shown in Figure 2.1. In short, it is a place of balancing confidence with vulnerability and making room for others (without judgment) to do the same.

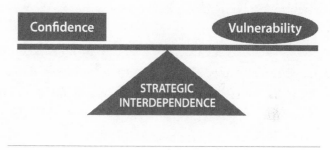

fig. 2.1

Let's see if we can't understand a little more about this first Strengths Strategy of choosing Strategic Interdependence and how it can help you in your life.

The Make-or-Break Factor

Before we dive in too far, let me first put a make-or-break factor on the table for your consideration, given its power to influence the relationship equation and your choice to be at Strategic Interdependence (or not). If you don't understand it, you'll end up being caught by its reverse energy and stuck in the Depletion Zone, given how deeply this make-or-break factor affects your performance. Additionally, if you are unaware of this factor, it will negatively impact every relationship in your life. It can even determine the degree to which you experience fulfillment and meaningful contribution, as well as the kind of happiness you long for in your work and in your life. It's huge! And you may have never even thought of it before, at least not in the way we speak of it here.

You can't change the reality of the make-or-break factor, but you can change your response to it, if you can see and understand it and leverage it for what it is. Here it is in just seven short words: *You are living in a bumper-car world.* This is the factor that you will either see and maximize to the advantage of yourself and others or become trapped by. Let's look at how this happens.

Whether you have experienced an actual bumper-car ride at your local carnival or not, you can likely envision a similarity between it and the way you "bump" people every day, or they bump you. Think about it like this. Every day you find yourself interacting with others, engaging with them, and having them flow in and out of your energy and performance and vice versa. These experiences can jar you unexpectedly and bump you up or down. All the while, simultaneously, you are bumping others up or down by your feelings and actions, whether you are aware of it or not. Sometimes it is wonderful and fun, and other times not so much.

For example, if you are like most people, you have routine negative bumper-car encounters with some people who likely make you just a little crazy—so much so that after you bump into them you might wish there were something like a "bumper-downer" car wash that would remove all the residual negative energy left in their wake. You may notice how much you dislike the way you feel after they leave. For example, you probably feel a little depleted, possibly even defeated, or just plain frustrated by the experience of engaging with them.

By the way, these feelings show that choosing Strategic Interdependence is *not* happening! Your life experience has likely taught you that without some real forethought and a clear strategy (maybe even a Strengths Strategy), your unchecked feelings or actions can fuel the downward spiral for you and for others.

Interestingly, this bumper-downer experience happens for you whenever you are unknowingly caught in one of these three ways of being:

- The Victim (also known as Dependent)
- The Hero (also known as Independent)
- The Player (also known as Codependent)

Let's run through a brief description of each so you can get a good sense of what these are like when they show up in your life. Let's start by discovering what it's like when you or others are caught in a state of being dependent, or The Victim.

The Victim

If you are like most people, it may be hard to think of yourself spending much time here. But you probably drift here more than you realize, even if it is only in your thoughts. This is the most natural place to go when you have unmet expectations of others and when those things start to get under your skin.

You'll recognize that you are here because you feel mad at others for not providing something you need, and you likely expect them to know automatically what it is. By the way, when The Victim shows up, you will also expect others to do whatever comes easily to you. For example, if you sense others' feelings easily, you will expect that they pay attention to your feelings and needs. If they don't, you might think they don't care about you and are inherently unworthy of your trust. Never mind whether they can sense your feelings and needs! When you operate from Dependence, this is not factored into the equation, and when your expected outcomes don't show up (and you think they should have), you feel angry, impatient, or judgmental.

Sometimes you are here because you don't know what to do or you don't have the answer. You also feel uncertain about other people around you and how they act. When this happens, you can get stuck waiting for someone or something to happen so you can see what to do or so you can feel safe or comfortable enough to engage. You might even blame others when you're unhappy or unsure.

"You should" is the belief going on here. When you get stuck at Dependence, you unknowingly hold a mind-set of "you serve me," as shown in Table 2.1.

Table 2.1—The Victim

See	Mantra: "You serve me." Belief: "You should."
Feel	Justified; situationally unconfident (don't know what to do); vulnerable; not responsible for what is happening
Do	Wait; withdraw; look outside self to explain why the problem is happening and what the solution should be
Get	Low energy and performance (and create the same for others); unfulfilled relationships; poor results; a distinct absence of meaning and purpose

This is not a productive or desirable place to engage from. Yet you can be caught here from time to time if you are not aware of the attributes.

The Hero

It's true that Dependence creates a bumper-downer experience for all involved. And, while you may think that being Independent is better, the truth is, it almost always leads to loneliness, disconnection, and burnout.

You know you are at Independence when you subconsciously hope to be the star of the story, to find the solution, and to solve the problem. It's also possible that others would say you don't listen well and that you talk over them or down to them. Here you feel like the expert and somehow obligated to share your vast wisdom.

When you operate from Independence, I'm also betting that you have a strong dislike for revealing your weakness to others. More than likely, you want to be seen by others as strong. You just do it yourself, rely on your own abilities, and don't let your guard down too much or trust others. You are likely holding an "I should" belief, complete with its self-judgment and negative self-talk when you are falling short of your own expectations. You no doubt hold the assumption here that "if it is to be, it is up to me."

It's also possible you don't know you are operating from a place of "I serve me" when you are here. Most likely you aren't intending to be selfish. You just get caught up chasing your own energy and performance, making sure that you get your work done, succeed, feel strong, and look good, with little or no awareness of your impact on others.

When you are playing The Hero, you are operating in a

silo and don't realize your impact. You might even feel and act sometimes like the whole world is on your shoulders and no one can handle it quite as well as you can. You can also become frustrated by the heavy load you carry, even though it is self-created, as shown in Table 2.2.

Table 2.2—The Hero

See	Mantra: "I serve me." Belief: "I should."
Feel	Often frenetic; trust in yourself but not others; unwilling to be vulnerable; hyper-responsible
Do	Multitask excessively; show up in "expert" mode (talking down or at others, not listening well); look to yourself to explain why something is happening or what the solution should be; try to control what is unfolding
Get	Short-term burst of energy or performance for yourself, but eventual burnout/negative impact on others; unfulfilled relationships; lack of meaning or purpose; less effective results than you might get if others could add their brilliance to the equation

You can see that although this can start out feeling good, it ends up in mediocrity and ultimately deteriorates to the Depletion Zone. And you may be entirely oblivious to it!

The Player

Now let's turn our attention to Codependence, a way of being that is akin to "I'll take care of you if you'll take care of me." You likely would not think of someone (especially yourself) operating from this place as The Player, but Codependence can be deceptive. Here you are unknowingly in a relationship "game" with someone or a group. And it is often one where the way you (or others) are being treated, or how the group is engaging, is not right, and you don't do anything about it. In that sense, you are equally The Player, because you are playing the "game" and you won't stop, even when it goes against your better judgment. Your fear of rocking the boat and your need for belonging and the approval of others are usually what keep you in this mode.

Table 2.3 shows the perfect example of living out the Codependence mantra, which is: "I serve you, so you'll serve me." It's a transactional relationship with informal agreements, kind of like "I'll agree with (or stay with) you, as long as you agree with (or stay with) me." This can sneak in, and you can too easily ignore your own conscience, or certain people, because they don't have anything to offer you—or because they are completely different from you, and you don't think they would play the "game" that keeps you supposedly safe and feeling important. This can quickly turn into an "Us vs. Them" scenario, as you can well imagine.

Additionally, when you look around at where Codependence exists in our world today, you might notice how it can be about the loudest voices winning and about dissing those who disagree (think political or social issues, for example). It can also become about popularity, worrying about how many followers you have on social media or how many comments you got on your Facebook post. If you get caught in thinking like this, you can bet that Codependence is the mindset you are holding in that moment.

Table 2.3—The Player

See	Mantra: "I serve you so that you will serve me." Belief: "I'll take care of you but only as long as you take care of me."
Feel	Unfulfilled; somewhat alone in a crowd; afraid to disrupt the pattern; false or low confidence in self or others; unwillingness to demonstrate vulnerability or uncertainty
Do	Behave inauthentically in words and actions; support negative behaviors of others; avoid tough conversations; ignore your own inner voice until it can no longer be heard
Get	Low-to-moderate energy and performance for yourself and others; unhappy relationships; the absence of real meaning/purpose

You may not think you are here often, but I bet you'd be surprised to realize you are likely here more than you think. Imagine if you had a Codependence alarm go off whenever you showed up here, so you could have the immediate feedback of knowing. Or maybe, more appropriately, a Depletion Zone alarm that would alert you that you were going down and a change was needed. Wouldn't that be something?

Becoming a "Bumper-Upper"

Now, you don't have to be Einstein to recognize that all three of these options ultimately provide a one-way ticket to low energy and terrible performance. Remember the Monopoly game? *Do not pass Go. Do not collect $200. Go straight to Jail.* That's pretty much what it feels like when you land in the Depletion Zone—like you've missed a turn or two when you choose Dependence, Independence, or Codependence. When you are in this zone, it feels like you are sitting out, looking in, and missing out on purpose, meaning, enjoyment, fulfillment, and connection. Or alternatively, like you are sitting there and inventing counterfeits of these things, hoping they can compensate for whatever you are missing.

Whether you know it or not, you are likely 100 percent familiar with each of these places and have your own love-hate relationship with them. It's not easy choosing Strategic Interdependence and becoming a "bumper-upper." To help you get to the point of cultivating the self-awareness needed and making the hard choices connected with Strategic Interdependence, let's look for patterns in the mantras connected to The Victim, The Hero, and The Player. Recognizing them can help you avoid being trapped by them yourself. The three mantras are:

- "You serve me" (Dependence).
- "I serve me" (Independence).
- "I serve you so that you'll serve me" (Codependence).

You don't have to look hard to find two glaring patterns. First, all three are focused on "serve me." The second thing is that these approaches don't lift you toward being a bumper-upper. If you look at these mantras together, realizing what they are about, you might feel like a little life gets sucked out of you just thinking about them. Clearly, we need an alternative!

Lucky for you, a hopeful alternative exists for anyone willing to choose Strategic Interdependence. The ultimate bumper-upper chooses a way of being that we call The Synergizer.

The Synergizer

When you choose to become The Synergizer you are choosing the deepest, most challenging, most mature response you are capable of. This choice is not easy. You choose to let go of judgment both of yourself and others. You also step fully into unconditional curiosity, which gives you permission to forge ahead into your unknown and untapped potential. You are a servant of others when you are here, following the opposite mantra of the other three places. Instead of focusing on "serve me," the Interdependence mantra is: "I serve us so we can serve others."

Here you look to contribute to something bigger than yourself. You stop waiting for others to take care of you and taking the whole world on your shoulders as though you are the only one who can do it. You also take responsibility for your own needs and frustrations, as well as your impact on others. These things all help you stay in a servant role and have your own cup full enough to share with others.

Finally, when you operate from Strategic Interdependence, you are not afraid of your weaknesses or of having them be revealed, since the "us" equation compensates for individual weaknesses, as shown in Table 2.4. This allows you to live with confidence and vulnerability, where you can boldly proclaim, "I know what I am. I know what I'm not. And both are okay!" It also allows you to receive others without judgment when their weaknesses show up and to graciously equalize the equation with your humbly offered strengths.

Table 2.4—The Synergizer

See	Mantra: "I serve us so that we can serve others." (And you would consider yourself to be part of the "us" equation.) Belief: "I will contribute my strengths and receive where I am weak (without judgment), to make a difference for us and others."
Feel	Present; patient with yourself and others; connected; calm; confident
Do	Clarify needs; align purposes; appreciate (not judge) differences; offer unconditional curiosity; synergize; show a willingness to learn
Get	High energy and performance for yourself and others; fulfilling relationships and meaningful experiences; optimal outcomes and results

Clearly, Strategic Interdependence is the most desirable alternative of all the possibilities. And it is the only one that has a straight path that leads straight to the Optimal Zone.

A Simple Strategy to Jump-Start Your Strategic Interdependence

It's not easy to choose to be The Synergizer when the bumper-car world you live in is most often in bumper-downer mode. Once you get stuck in the magnetic pull toward the Depletion Zone, this pull can set off an internal reaction that leaves you feeling like you are "pinging" from one ineffective way of being to the next, almost as though you were the ball inside a pinball machine.

To put an end to this phenomenon and jump-start your Strategic Interdependence, you need to make some choices. The following three decisions form a simple but effective strategy that will help you shift toward Strategic Interdependence and out of the pinball machine:

- **Serve others first.** This includes choosing a mindset that is focused on serving others without expectation and not just yourself. "How can I serve here?" is the question that will anchor you when you feel called to "serve me" instead of others.

- **Give and receive.** This includes choosing to contribute your strengths to others, without judgment or fear and without fear of your weaknesses, mistakes, or failures. "What do I have to give, as well as receive, in this situation?" is the question that will anchor you when you feel worried about whether you are enough.

▸ **Be unconditionally curious.** This includes choosing to be open and unconditionally curious whenever the vast frontiers of your untapped potential call you into the frightening place of the Growth Zone. "What is wanting to be discovered here?" is the question that will anchor you when you feel you are leaving your Comfort Zone.

Consider for a moment what might happen if you could combine the power of these decisions. How might these choices Shift Up! your energy and performance? How would they affect others?

If you are willing to try them, you will find that the results speak for themselves. When you choose Strategic Interdependence, you are also choosing to create the conditions that allow you to be at your best. This means that your needed conditions are not left to outside-in happenstance. It also means that you begin to discover more of your own power to create conditions that will draw others toward the Optimal Zone with you—even people who have seemingly set up permanent residence in the Depletion Zone! If you are skeptical, check out what it takes to become the catalyst to shift the relationship equation toward Strategic Interdependence, even with negative people.

Becoming the Catalyst

Let's finish this chapter by getting a clear picture of what the ultimate Synergizer is like in your opinion so you know what to aim for. To help you get there, take a second and think about the people you might characterize as the ultimate bumper-uppers. Who are they? What are they like? How would you describe them? My guess is that you know exactly who they are. When you've been with them, it's like a warm feeling that lingers even after they are gone. You feel stronger and a bit more optimistic for having been with them. They raise you up toward the Optimal Zone, and you simply enjoy being with them.

Now, it might excite you to know how you can be one of these people, but only if you understand this one little trick. It starts with the realization that every bumper-car interaction with others has an impact. You rub off and influence others, and they, in turn, rub off and influence you. This is what Mary Parker Follett meant when she said, "Various factors in a situation are continually influencing each other. I never react to you, but to 'you-plus-me' or to be more appropriate, it is 'I-plus-you' reacting to 'you-plus-me.'" (See Figure 2.2.)

The Synergizer knows this and uses it to make a difference. If others around you are caught in an outside-in, reactive way of being, you could be the outside-in catalyst that others react to. You can be the bumper-upper that can inspire their movement toward Strategic Interdependence and their individual choice to also Shift Up! Although your way of achieving this outcome is likely not what you might think.

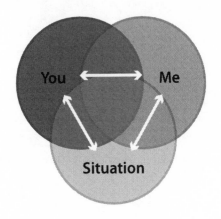

fig. 2.2

It's not about technique. It's not about learning skills and doing it right. The truth is that it is not exactly any one specific thing that you would *do* that would make a difference. It is that you would *be* different, and that is the difference! Your way of being can be the way out of the Depletion Zone for others. If you think about it, you realize that some people have never truly had a bumper-upper role model in their lives, and you could be the first. Your choice to make decisions preemptively to change the equation begins a whole new kind of bumper-car experience, one that wraps others up in a consistent, positive experience until it starts to sink in. Let me offer a simple equation to help you see what I mean.

Imagine that your work requires you to associate with someone who is routinely negative. He or she brings to your exchange a "-1" virtually every time, as this person subtracts from the equation. If you respond to this person in kind, with similar bumper-downer feelings, thoughts, or actions, you also add a "-1," which factors significantly into the "Us" output of the equation. You see, if you also choose "-1," then you have guaranteed a negative result, and both of you end up in the Depletion Zone. Just so you can see it, if you add your "-1" to the "-1" of the other person, the overall equation and result look something like Figure 2.3.

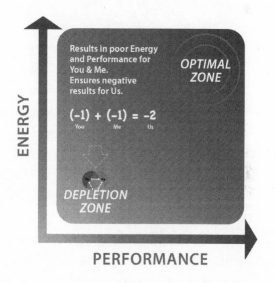

fig. 2.3

Now, you don't have to be a math wizard to figure out what happens if you have already made the choices we have outlined here and decided how you'll respond when the "-1" gets thrown into the equation with you. Think about how it could be to review these questions when you are teetering on whether you will get caught back in the pinball machine or whether you will instead be The Synergizer. When you ask yourself the following questions, notice how it changes your entire focus and how much easier it is to choose Strategic Interdependence:

▸ How can I serve here?

▸ What do I have to give, as well as receive, in this situation?

▸ What possibilities are waiting to be discovered here?

This means that you would insert a new element into the equation, a "+1" instead of a "-1," which changes the whole equation. The moment you add a "+1," you have just canceled out all the negativity in the "Us" outcome, bumping you up out of the Depletion Zone, as shown in Figure 2.4. This does not automatically take the other person straight to the Optimal Zone, but a step into the Development Zone™ is still a step up— and a step in the right direction.

It's so simple, really. First, you lift the other person before you even have a bumper-car encounter with them by deciding your responses in advance. These choices, in turn, lift you and every person who will ever bump into you. Then you lift the other person (and yourself) when you choose to honor your predetermined responses. This way even if the other person does not enthusiastically Shift Up! right away, you can still have a positive impact. And perhaps in time, as your bumper-upper experiences continue and they watch you model a new way of thinking and being, maybe they, too, will eventually make new choices.

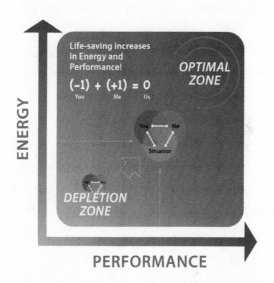

fig. 2.4

Like Chris Williams did for Cameron White, you can be the guide, the person who changes the trajectory of someone's entire existence. You can Shift Up! for them and for yourself countless times by choosing Strategic Interdependence. You may never know the impact you have!

Are you ready to make some preemptive choices?

Growth Zone Challenge: Power Points to See and Shift From

Welcome back to the **Growth Zone Challenge**. I invite you to think about where your breakthrough insights have come from in this chapter and how you will use them to further your growth. Study the list that follows and notice: *Which of the following was your biggest takeaway? What is one thing you will do differently to act on what you have learned? And with whom will you share your learning and commitment?*

▸ You are living in a bumper-car world where others tend to respond from an outside-in, reactive mode. You can use this to your advantage as you shift your own mind-set and way of being toward becoming a bumper-upper catalyst.

▸ Four different bumper-car interactions are possible. You can respond as The Victim (Dependent), The Hero (Independent), The Player (Codependent), or The Synergizer (Interdependent). The first three are focused on "serving me" and result in bumper-downer engagement, whereas Strategic Interdependence is focused on "serving us" and "serving others," and bumps you and others up.

▸ Choosing Strategic Interdependence happens before you ever encounter anyone or any difficult situation. It is a function of preemptively making three choices that guide all interactions: serving others first, giving and receiving, and being unconditionally curious. Each choice has a specific question that will prompt you to make the choice again, when your resolve is tested.

Shift Up! through Leveraging Success Patterns™

> You have had successes and you have had failures, and from them both Optimal and Depletion Zone patterns have become part of your life. The only question that remains is which pattern will have more power in the moment of choice.
>
> —LISA GREGORY, MS, CPAC

Many years ago, I received a call from an unfamiliar out-of-state number. Normally, I would have let it go to voice mail when I was working, but I decided to take it that day. I'm so glad I did, because that phone call changed my whole life and the trajectory of my career. On the other end of the line was one of the highest-energy people I have ever talked to, just waiting for me to pick up.

Jen spoke fast. She was crisp in her intent, and once she introduced herself as a senior leader of a large financial firm, she turned immediately to her purpose. I was a bit surprised that someone from such a large company was contacting me, especially given that I was several thousand miles away and a relatively new coach. I recognized the company name and knew this was the "real deal," the kind of contact every coach eventually hopes to be ready for.

She gave me the bottom-line story of one of her direct reports named Laura, who was a manager in her fast-paced, execution-driven organization, and then explained that this woman was failing miserably, and the organization was ready to send her packing. However, they had compassionately decided on one last recourse. They agreed to hire a coach to "fix" her as part of her last-ditch performance plan. Apparently, I was the person recommended for the job, although I didn't quite have the heart to tell her I wasn't in the market to "fix" anyone. I wisely decided to save that explanation for another day.

You should also know this was the first time I was contacted by anyone outside of rural Minnesota, where I spent the beginning years of my career, and I was trying to be excited about the call. But a mounting anxiety and nagging fear got in the way. I'd never experienced such a large firm or worked with leaders in upper management from a company this size. I simply felt like I had no frame of reference to know where to begin or even how to think about it.

All the same, as Jen spoke I took notes to calm my nerves. I asked questions, hoping to sound smart, and tried to get clear about what her needs and desired outcomes were. I found she could spell out her exact goals in black-and-white terms, including specific measures for each objective. And I told myself to just keep breathing as I listened to her rattle off her tidy list. When she was done and I had exhausted my questions, Jen asked me what I thought. I can't explain what happened next, since it certainly did not reflect the apprehension I felt. I found myself explaining that I would be thrilled to take on this assignment, but only under one condition. As I said that, there was an audible "Oh?" on the other end of the line. I guess she had not expected that from me.

I gulped, and with as much confidence as I could muster, I said to her, "I'm happy to coach Laura, but only if I also get to coach you." That was when my sarcastic inside voice taunted me a little and said, *Wow! Did you just say that?*

At this point, Jen was backpedaling—and fast—and I thought I may have just messed up the one and only real coaching opportunity I would ever get outside of Backwoods, USA. In an authoritative voice, she explained that she did not need coaching, that she did not have time for it, and that her performance as a leader was just fine. Not wanting to upset her, my gentle response was simple: If things were going to shift for Laura, part of what had to shift was the relationship equation between the two of them. My instinct told me that if Laura was worried about their relationship, it would unconsciously drain her energy rather than focus it on improvement. I was lucky this made enough sense for her to grudgingly agree to my terms, although she was clearly not happy about it.

That was when a whole new chapter opened in my life and in both of theirs as well, leading to what seemed like a miraculous transformation in all three of us. Nearly a year later, I was on a plane heading to be with them for one final coaching session. I couldn't believe that our coaching experience was almost over, and I found myself quietly reflecting with wonder and joy on what had transpired and on how far each of us had come. The next day we would bring closure to what had become one of the biggest high points and milestones of my entire career.

As the sun was just beginning to dip below the horizon, I was reveling in the view from the plane and found myself thinking about that first phone call. I got tough with myself that day when I realized that all my fear and negative self-talk meant that I was stuck in a "serve me" pattern. I could see the selfishness in that. My need to be liked had become more important than offering up my gifts to serve with my heart wide open. I kept thinking about Henry Wadsworth Longfellow's statement to "give what you have. To someone, it may be better than you dare think." I didn't know everything, but I knew that I knew enough. I just needed to get clear on what I did have to give them and anchor in that.

I think that was the moment when the Strengths Strategy of Leveraging Success Patterns began to show up with intention in my life. I started to coach myself that day, like I was my own client, and began to look for patterns of effectiveness in things I was doing or unique ways of being in past experiences. I wrote my patterns down. What I discovered was that one of my most effective strategies was the exact thing I was doing in that moment: evaluating success patterns and finding new ways to reapply them.

I started comparing events, it was clear that whenever I

looked at myself with a kind and appreciative lens, celebrating the things I was doing right, I could always serve others better. The negative patterns that caused me to spiral downward were strong enough that they could easily overtake my thoughts if I was not intentional about making a different choice. This revelation boosted my confidence because I realized I could choose which patterns I wanted to activate: I could flip the switch up and move toward the Optimal Zone as I called on my success patterns, or I could flip it down and drop into frustration, moving into the Depletion Zone. I don't know why that seemed like a novel thought to me, but it sure excited me.

The experience also motivated me to begin practicing Leveraging Success Patterns with much greater intention and frequency, especially when I noticed I was in a downward spiral. I'd never fully realized until that moment that I always had the key to get out of being stuck. This insight was so freeing! It felt a bit like the sun had begun to slowly rise after a long, dark night, revealing the most awe-inspiring world with color, light, and new, amazing views. It seemed to amplify my ability to see, and I felt like I was noticing everything, especially other people, with more clarity.

This helped me with Laura, as I was better able to see and appreciate the things that made her unique and brilliant as a leader. I remember one session when we were working through a specific experience she was battling and looking for how her strengths might help her. As I listened to her, I felt a warmth explode from my heart, which seemed to almost envelop my whole body. I was genuinely in awe of her humble, sensitive, and authentic leadership style. She was so real. She cared so much for her young, inexperienced team and rejoiced in cheerleading them to success. I found her to be so willing to receive others, to give them room to be big, because she didn't need to be. Her unique package of gifts was beautiful to me.

What surprised me, though, was that she honestly didn't seem to see these gifts or know how to hold this part of her. It was almost like it wasn't real to her. We continued to explore this, as we had been doing for many months. And I could only hope to keep holding up the mirror, listening, encouraging, and reflecting brilliance back to her until she could begin to see herself and trust what she was seeing. Toward the end of that session, she suddenly became quiet, and I could feel her wheels turning and gears grinding into place. That was when it happened! Light seemed to spring instantly into her eyes. It was as though she were seeing for the first time, and suddenly the whole world came into view. Oh, the joy on her face in that moment! It was there, right along with a deep, moving sense of humility that clearly enveloped her. She seemed so big and so small at the same time, and she positively glowed in the warmth of her new revelation.

That memory made me smile as I looked out the airplane window, the sun now gone from the sky. It caused me to wonder about tomorrow's meeting and how Jen, Laura's boss, would feel as her team's latest statistics were unveiled. Laura's numbers had steadily increased since the beginning of our work together. Her team was now showing a 90 percent improvement in productivity from where they were last year. I was pretty sure Jen would be excited about that! Not to mention the latest employee engagement scores were in, and Laura's team was near the top of the company.

What I wasn't yet sure of was whether Jen realized how Laura's change was in large measure due to her own shift. Not that Jen started out wanting to change, or even thinking she needed to, but change she did! It was quite amazing to see how her leadership had done a complete 180 once she realized that something more was possible. She was so Independent and competitive when we first started working together, but the moment she had a taste of the power of Strategic Interdependence and its ability to magnify her own capabilities and those of others, she was all in. There was no going back. She wanted results and was willing to become increasingly curious about herself and others.

I found myself remembering the day Jen realized her Independence negatively affected her relationships and expectations of others. She discovered how she expected her direct reports to all have the identical success patterns and strategies for optimal performance that she did. That took her back just a little. When she began to see how her expectations, along with her impatience and frustration, were hurting others' confidence, she became highly motivated to not just do different things but to *be* different. That was the day Jen became a real leader, the day when she chose to be a servant leader instead of a taskmaster. Servant leadership became the hallmark of her career from that point forward, and it was what she was known for in all the years following, particularly during the time she was the CEO of her company.

Servant leadership is also what Laura came to most appreciate her for, as I realized in the concluding moments of our last meeting together. Jen's face, now softened by her growing resolve and desire to lift others, shone with humble admiration as she looked directly into Laura's eyes. I would never have guessed a year earlier that I would hear these words from her, as she spoke with deep gratitude and genuine caring: "Laura, you have taught me what it means to be a leader and why celebrating the differences of others matters. I didn't realize how important this is. You've helped me learn how to capitalize on what makes each person special and how to help others be more of who they were born to be. This is real leadership! And I had missed that for so long. Thank you for being patient with me. I will never be the same again." She had a hint of moisture in her eyes, though she likely would not have wanted to admit it.

A miraculous Shift Up! will always follow when you search out success patterns to get out of the box you are stuck in.

In so many ways, Jen summarized what all of us had learned through each other. She reminded us that a miraculous Shift Up! will always follow when you search out success patterns to get out of the box you are stuck in. You have patterns of success and patterns of failure. The patterns you look for and focus on will be reflected by your results. If you want to shift performance (including the relationships that create it), shift your focus. Your performance will shift, because you will always see whatever you seek!

With that in mind, let's explore how Leveraging Success Patterns can help you Shift Up! and change your own focus, and how you can get yourself unstuck in those moments of negativity and positively affect your relationships and performance using this Strengths Strategy.

Shift Up! Your Focus

If you have lived for any amount of time on this planet, chances are you have been properly trained in a mind-set that will never produce optimal performance nor support the kind of relationships to create it. And you may be entirely unaware. The mindset we are referring to is called "deficit-thinking." It's what I demonstrated early in the story, complete with my inner voice knocking me down at every turn. You likely have your own negative voice in the back of your head and know exactly how it sounds! It's the voice telling you you're not enough and never will be and that you had better "fix" yourself and fast! It's the only way you'll ever be enough.

If you think about it, "fixing" is what you do to cars and broken windows and the garbage disposal when it doesn't work. It's not what you "do" to people and certainly isn't something you want to ever do to yourself, as this will take you right to the

Depletion Zone. It will also kill your performance and undermine every relationship that matters to you.

Maybe it's time to think differently, to understand strengths and weaknesses in a way that doesn't demand that you fix your weakness, or someone else's, so you can feel strong. The worry about weakness blinds you to your strengths and those of others. You can't see success patterns if you're focused on weaknesses. So, let's start by reframing the whole idea of weaknesses and strengths, including how to define them. Figure 3.1 offers a different way to think about strengths and weaknesses. Consider how you would define them based on what you see.

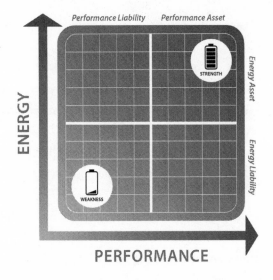

fig. 3.1

Notice that each of the circles in Figure 3.1 represents a strength or weakness, a thought pattern, behavior, or activity that leads you to high energy and performance (or its opposite). If what you are doing, or your way of being, leads you and others to experience high energy and high performance, you are engaging from strengths. If not, then you probably feel weak because you are engaging from a place of weakness.

Framing strengths and weaknesses this way invites you to think differently about them and can even help you know where to look to find them. For example, you may not have thought about the fact that you have "doing" strengths, which are all about the things you do to make a difference (like your ability to organize, memorize, solve problems, or listen deeply). You also have "being" strengths, which are about your way of being (like being patient, curious, encouraging, or persistent). Both kinds of strengths add great value to you and to others. And defining your strengths empowers you to look for both "doing" and "being" contributions when you mine your past successes for patterns.

Another important thing to realize is that neither strengths nor weaknesses are ever just about you, given the "bumper-car" world you live in. You always leave an imprint on others. If your way of "doing" or "being" depletes others, or has a negative effect on them, you are not having an experience of your strengths. For them, it will most certainly feel like you are displaying a weakness. This offers an invitation to think differently about the way you engage with yourself and others, ever mindful of your own impact.

The same thought patterns, behaviors, or activities that lift you to the Optimal Zone can also drag you to the Depletion Zone if you are not careful. Your strengths and weaknesses can easily be two sides of the same coin, meaning the thing you do well in one situation can become a liability in another. This can be an exciting revelation. However, this works only if you understand what the experience of strength looks like so you can call it up and customize it to fit new situations.

SEE Success Patterns to Optimize Outcomes

The Strengths Strategy of Leveraging Success Patterns will help you shift your focus from deficit-thinking and weakness-fixing toward a kinder strengths-oriented approach to yourself, others, and your situations. When you begin from a place of deficit-thinking ("What's wrong with me?"), you immediately shut down your access to your inner brilliance by worrying, "How can I 'fix' this?" When this happens, you stop yourself from being able to create new solutions to your problems. It can be the equivalent of a negative "bumper-downer" experience with an important authority figure in your life.

66

You are your most important authority figure.
You can either call your negative patterns into action
or tell yourself to flip the switch and Shift Up!, using
your success patterns to get there.

99

You are your most important authority figure. You can either call your negative patterns into action or tell yourself to flip the switch and Shift Up!, using your success patterns to get there. Remembering this saying can guide your focus: *Whichever you see is where you will be.* As seen in Figure 3.2, if you focus on weakness, you'll head straight to the Depletion Zone. Conversely, if you look for strengths, you'll find yourself magnetized toward the Optimal Zone.

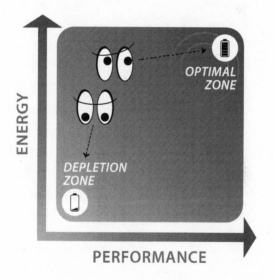

fig. 3.2

Once you choose your focus, the hard part is over. But you are not finished. Seeing differently is more than just looking around. It's also about diving deeper into your patterns so you can see them and choose to use them for good. By the way, "SEE" is an acronym I created to guide you through the SEE and Shift Up! process. SEE stands for:

- ▸ Strengths-mining past successes
- ▸ Envisioning your possibilities
- ▸ Evolving your solution

Let's review each of these and then walk through a real-life example of how this strategy works.

Strengths-Mining Past Successes

Strengths-mining past successes is exactly what it sounds like. It is about mining your past experiences while looking for strengths patterns. The most impactful experiences are those in which you managed to escape frustration and moved up and out of the negativity. You can mine these situations by asking two specific questions that reveal your "doing" and "being" strengths:

- ▸ What was I "doing" to get out (of the negative situation)?
- ▸ What was my way of "being" (and how did it help me)?

Answering these questions is hard work. This process reveals unique patterns of strength at work in your life. When you answer them, they awaken new energy and confidence to face the vulnerability of the downward spiral you are in.

You can remember this step with this saying: "See your best to find your rest." And "rest" in this context has two meanings. First, you experience rest from the magnetic pull of deficit-thinking. Second, you are empowered to see the rest of your possibilities. Through practicing this first step, you will find that strengths-mining becomes a gateway to unknown potential where you can find new and empowering solutions.

Envisioning Your Possibilities

Envisioning possibilities is an invitation to cross from your known possibilities to your untapped potential. This requires stepping courageously into being an explorer of the endless frontier within you by using your imagination. Here you envision a future where you have solved whatever problem has prompted your searching and the ideal results you have created. Not surprisingly, you are going to explore "doing" and "being" contributions again, thinking about them as though you were right there observing yourself:

▸ What am I "doing" to create amazing results?

▸ What is my way of "being" as I contribute here?

As you think about your results, actions, and way of being as though you have already arrived at them, you'll feel additional energy and hope. It even feels a little bit like you are finding your flow and rhythm, and you are awakening to new ways of solving your current problem. To help you remember this step, consider this saying: "Think 'as though' to find your flow."

Evolving Your Solution

This important step recognizes that no two situations are exactly alike, and what created success before may not necessarily create it again. When you confidently integrate the best from the past with imagined possibilities for the future, you can approach a new solution with Confident Vulnerability™ and search for a brand-new solution. It answers two questions, as you think about "doing" and "being" different to contribute to the solution:

- ▸ What one to three things will I "do" daily to make a difference?
- ▸ How do I choose to "be" in this situation?

Our purpose here is all about creating a new ending to a tired old story by drawing your past successes and future possibilities into a cohesive whole. Don't be surprised if you feel more whole and a little less fractured afterward. This is one of the many outcomes associated with this step. To help you remember this step, think of this saying: "Find the blend to create a new end."

Leveraging Success Patterns in Action

When you look at these three steps together, what do you notice? What situation or challenge are you presently facing where a Strengths Strategy like this would be useful? To help you see how this strategy works, I'll share my own real-life experience of this tool and model it, using one of the experiences I recalled in my strengths-mining exercise in the Jen/Laura story (when I was looking for success patterns). As we walk through this example, you may wish to think about how this Strengths Strategy could also work for you.

Strengths-Mining Past Successes

You can't activate the first step in the SEE and Shift-Up! process until you choose it. Usually the pain or frustration of being caught in a negative spiral and not knowing how to get out will prompt you to SEE and Shift Up! Sometimes, though, it can take days, weeks, months, or, in my case, years to figure it out.

For example, early in my marriage, my husband and I were gifted with an unusual daughter who has blessed our lives in countless ways. But her gifts came with a giant price tag, including a large dose of heartache. Our daughter was born with a disability known as spina bifida, which meant she had some paralysis in her legs and feet. She also had mental impairment, vision challenges, and a long list of medical issues to battle. By the time she was three, she had endured nearly ten surgeries and had spent close to 20 percent of her life in the hospital. She also was in pain most of the time.

The mother within me ached every day. I felt responsible for her disability. I also felt enormous guilt over my inability to relieve her suffering, to create a positive life for her, and to stay connected to her, given how deep her suffering was. My empathy sometimes created a barrier to joyfully loving her, since I was often overwhelmed by her suffering. Additionally, I was clearly stuck in a deficit-oriented story, with no foreseeable way to "fix" the situation. It meant that I spent a lot of time feeling depressed and sad. As a result, my relationships at home suffered, along with my performance in graduate school and at work.

Recognizing the Need to SEE and Shift Up!

I knew something needed to shift, so I decided to step away for an afternoon to gain perspective and comfort. I went hiking high in Utah's beautiful Uinta Mountains near where we lived. There, I found myself sitting above the gorgeous emerald-green waters of Tibble Fork Reservoir and considering what was unfolding. As I closed my eyes and leaned back against a pine tree and became still, an image began to unfold in my mind. As I focused on the image, I saw a lifeless prison cell. What became even more horrifying was that there, in the corner, helplessly curled up, I saw myself—with my arms wrapped tightly around my legs and my head resting defeatedly on my knees. The confinement was oppressive, almost as if I could hardly breathe. The air seemed thin and empty, and the darkness seemed to stifle all hope.

Then I looked deeper. To my surprise, I discovered the prison door was wide open and no one guarded the entrance! It was as if I had voluntarily confined myself to the darkest corner of that cell, perhaps, in a way, as a punishment for my perceived failure to stop my daughter's pain and make things all better. Although it appeared I could leave, I had no idea how to do it.

Discovering Past "Doing" and "Being" Contributions

Sitting in the stillness, the energy of the mountains and water seemed to fuel me. It inspired me to remember a similar time, when I had made peace with a deep loss that took me almost ten years to process. I remembered the details of my own trans-formation and thought carefully about what happened to create the change. I asked myself these questions and thought about my answers carefully:

What was I "doing" to get out?	What was my way of "being"?
I took time alone to walk in nature.	I was connected to and energized by nature.
I became my best friend. I asked questions like, "What happened here? Why do I think something needs to change?"	I was nonjudgmental, honest, uncon-ditionally curious, and in friendship with myself.
I went toward the loss (rather than away from it) by asking, "What am I feeling? Why?"	I comforted myself by being empa-thetic, kind, gentle, and soothing.

When I moved through the memory, I felt a surprising peace settle over me. The ache began to give way to a hopeful remem-brance, one that gave me permission to believe that my current experience was temporary. *What if I could write a new ending to this story?* I found myself wondering and granting myself permis-sion to think about what that story could look like.

Envisioning Your Possibilities

I started to envision a new future by seeing myself feeling and responding quite differently. I could see myself doing things differently with my daughter and see a different way of being with myself and with her. The more I thought about it, the more real it seemed.

Envisioning Future "Doing" and "Being" Contributions

What will I "do" to create amazing results?	What will my way of "being" be here?
I will look at my daughter as someone who is strong, confident, and capable. I will celebrate her strengths every day. I will notice what is possible for her by embracing those possibilities rather than trying to "fix" her.	I will focus on strengths rather than weaknesses. I will be appreciative, celebratory of small steps and tiny victories, and a mirror of her brilliance so she, too, can see it.
I will coach her to help her see and use her own strengths differently with strengths-mining, envisioning, and evolving solutions.	I will be lovingly fierce and compassionate without coddling her. I will ask more than I tell by staying curious. And I will trust her ability to find her own answers.
I will give her permission to be authentic about her weakness, to not know, to be okay with struggling, and to speak candidly about it with others and to teach them how she works.	I will offer transparency without embarrassment. I will be confident and vulnerable and be okay with both.

After thinking like this for a while, I realized that the more I let my mind go to the possibilities, the more I could see. I also noticed I didn't feel curled up in the corner of the prison cell anymore. I was outside! I was blinking in the sunlight, wondering why I had stayed there so long.

Evolving Your Solution

On some level, I knew that for this to be real I had to decide on some specific actions to guide my daily focus so as to avoid the downward Depletion spiral. I needed to *do* some things differently. I needed to *be* different. I felt ready to commit to actions that would help me to take baby steps, right along with her halting, crooked steps. I made some critical decisions that day that became part of our relationship. Here is what they were.

Choosing Present "Doing" and "Being" Contributions

What one to three specific things are you "doing" daily?	How are you choosing to "be"?
I notice my own frustration and recognize it as a signal that I have forgotten my choices. If it surfaces, I apologize and acknowledge my own weakness.	I am kind, unconditionally curious, and authentic with her and myself. I see and accept weakness without judgment or worry that either of us is not enough.

Continued

I watch for, and share with her, every evidence I see of her strengths and abilities showing up in the smallest degree—at least one time each day.	I am strengths-oriented and leverage every possible advantage to help her grow.
I ask curious questions to help us get unstuck rather than talk down to her or tell her what to do or how to be.	I am unconditionally curious. I trust our inner strength to emerge. I stay to find new and better responses so we both can grow.

As I walked down the mountain and back to my car, I felt different, lighter. My head was clearer. My heart was less burdened. I was almost even a tiny bit excited to begin again and see what new endings to our story we could write together. I was liking this story a whole lot better than the one I started with!

The Rest of the Story

This is not a complicated process. It's quite simple, really. You just look at your past successes, your ideal future, and your present possibilities and identify your "doing" and "being" contributions in each place. Each step in the process gives you momentum and strength for the next one. Gradually you start to notice how your experience of weakness begins to Shift Up! It starts with one action, consistently delivered over time, and the next thing you know, your past stumbling block has become a stepping-stone to a new future.

I know it was for me. Three years after that momentous day on the mountaintop, I stood at the finish line with other parents at my daughter's first Special Olympics. This was a meaningful event because she—the little girl who was never supposed to walk—was about to run the 100-yard dash! She was noticeably different from the other disabled children, particularly in her plastic braces and her cumbersome twister cables keeping her feet straight. All the other athletes had learned to walk as toddlers. This tenacious little girl had learned to walk not just once as a late-blooming preschooler but three different times, given the various orthopedic surgeries she'd had to undergo.

I had decided ahead of time that I didn't care about the outcome of the race. As the racers took their mark, I knew it was enough for me that she embodied the Special Olympics creed, which she had been talking about and sharing for days in anticipation of this event: *"Let me win, but if I cannot win, let me be brave in the attempt."*

The gun sounded, and the runners were off. She was looking at me through big Coke-bottle glasses strapped to her head, with the goofiest grin on her face as she started. But fifteen yards in, the grin was gone, and she was huffing and puffing as if she was halfway through a marathon. Her arms were pumping faster than her legs could move.

It was like a scene from a movie. I imagined the *Chariots of Fire* soundtrack blasting in the background, creating a dramatic effect as she did her best to race down the track. I'll never forget the pride I felt watching her run, rejoicing in the miracle that she could run at all, even as halting as her steps were.

That was when the unexpected happened. In an unusual and unforgettable turn of events, she pushed herself nearly to her breaking point and burst ahead of the Down's syndrome boy in the next lane. She won the race by a foot. And you would have thought she was the champion of the world the way she exploded with joy as she fell into my arms, with tears running down her cheeks. I won't lie. She wasn't the only one with tears in her eyes.

She was my hero that day. And twenty-five years later, she still is, as she has passed every mile marker that psychologists and doctors told us she would never reach, living on her own, holding down a job, and living a joyful life of quiet contribution. She is a living, breathing, walking example of Leveraging Success Patterns every day, in case you were wondering if this Strengths Strategy works.

If it can work for a little disabled girl and her differently-abled mother, then it can work for you too. It can stop the negative spiral and change your focus and energy so you Shift Up! It will give you confidence as you realize you are the person who flips the switch and decides which direction you'll move toward to live with your heart open and escape your self-made prison.

Are you ready to SEE and Shift Up? Are you ready to find the success patterns that can change your life and future? Well, you're in luck, because this is the Strengths Strategy that can help you do just that!

Growth Zone Challenge: Power Points to See and Shift From

Welcome back to the **Growth Zone Challenge.** I invite you to think about where your breakthrough insights have come from in this chapter and how you will use them to further your growth. Study the list that follows and notice: *Which of the following was your biggest takeaway? What is one thing you will do differently to act on what you have learned? And with whom will you share your learning and commitment?*

▸ You have patterns of success and patterns of failure. Whichever patterns you look for and focus on will be reflected by your results (either in the Depletion Zone or Optimal Zone). If you want to shift performance (including the relationships that create it), shift your focus.

▸ "Fixing" is something you do to cars, windows, and garbage disposals when they are broken, not to people. If you get stuck focusing on weakness, you cannot see your own or others' strengths.

▸ A strength is nothing more than a thought pattern, behavior, or activity that leads to high energy and performance for you and others. On the other hand, a weakness is a thought pattern, behavior, or activity that leads to low energy or performance for you and others.

▸ Leveraging Success Patterns is a life-changing way to SEE your "doing" and "being" contributions differently from the perspective of—

▷ **S**trengths-mining past successes

▷ **E**nvisioning your possibilities

▷ **E**volving your solution

Shift Up! through Intelligently Influencing Others™

When the tide rises, all ships rise, too. When you rise by making the choices needed to Shift Up!, others rise with you, too. You automatically influence others when you positively influence yourself.

—STEVE JEFFS, TOP 50 GLOBAL LEADERSHIP COACH

By all outside appearances, Nolan and Elizabeth seemed to have a storybook life and family. Nolan's career had taken him into influential roles, including inside a handful of well-respected Fortune 500 companies. His peers, leaders, and direct reports, not to mention his many friends, viewed him as extremely intelligent, generous, and highly successful. So did his wife, who would have added that though he was not tall, she surely thought of him as dark and handsome. He seemed to have it all together in ways that were downright enviable.

Elizabeth, a well-known opera star, seemed to be his equal in every way. She had sung in the finest concert halls across the globe, including Carnegie Hall and the State Opera House in Vienna. To hear her sing was like listening to an angel! Her refined elegance reminded me of Princess Diana. She even looked like her, complete with delicate features and almost tear-drop-shaped eyes that drew you in and filled you with warmth the moment she caught you in her view. Elizabeth was kind and gentle as well as charismatic and inspiring. Yet she was also resolute and down-to-earth. I doubt you would ever feel as though she were "above" you, if you were lucky enough to meet her, even though it would be easy to believe otherwise.

What made Nolan and Elizabeth even more inspiring was that, despite her world travels and his often caring for their children in single-parent style, they also showed up in a family-of-the-year-like way. They taught their children together whenever they could, and they served outside the home together, both in their church and at local charities, whenever they had the chance. You could see how involved they were in their children's intellectual, social, and character development by the respectful and loving way the children interacted with others and the obvious affection between them and their parents. Additionally, you could see the fruits of their strong family in the children's humble self-assurance, their clean-cut appearance, and their kindness and awareness of others, not to mention their confident mastery of unique talents that set them apart.

Now, here is where the story gets a little interesting. Appearances can be quite deceiving, as I learned during my time working with them. Elizabeth was experiencing an increase in her extensive travel, and Nolan took on a new role that required their family to move. This happened right as their youngest daughter developed some new chronic health issues.

As the stress in the situation mounted, it became apparent that beneath all the success indicators, their marriage was quietly eroding. Elizabeth wore a mask to cover up an increasingly empty and lonely heart. And Nolan, who had a marshmallow heart, seemed to be sinking into the feeling of failure. He started avoiding Elizabeth as much as possible, which only compounded the problem. They were soon caught in a deadlock and couldn't see how to get out.

In thinking about your own relationships, maybe you've had something similar in your own life. Like Nolan and Elizabeth, perhaps you wanted your relationship to be close again after a period of struggle and to just feel connected. Or perhaps like them, your intentions were also good, and the problem was not about the depth of commitment to the relationship. Additionally, if you are anything like most people having relationship challenges, you have probably created what you thought was a perfect formula to turn the relationship around. This is also what Nolan and Elizabeth did, each with their own ideas about what needed to happen so that things could be back in flow. Not surprisingly, both wanted to influence the other to accept their formula. Does any of this sound familiar?

I have a hunch it might, because their story is the human story of relationship breakdown and the classic expectations of how to "fix" an apparently broken relationship. I have emphasized the word "fix" here in part to call your mind back to what happens when you try to fix relationships the way you fix your plumbing when it isn't working. Using weakness-fixing (or deficit-thinking) to increase the positive flow in relationships is like trying to fix your toilet with a plunger when you need a plumbing snake. Just as you may need different tools for different plumbing problems, you may need a different approach—maybe even a Strengths Strategy—to influence others intelligently and to increase the positive flow in your relationships. A weakness-fixing mind-set will never create intelligent influence.

Let's see if we can discover what *will* create intelligent influence and what that is all about.

Intelligent Influence

It is interesting to consider that influence and intelligent influence are not the same. For starters, the outcomes are not necessarily the same. How you experience them is not the same, and your way of being is not at all the same when you are in them. If you have never considered their differences before, you might be a little intrigued by using this as a backdrop for our discussion here, given the rich insights you will find by taking a closer look.

If you're like me, you can get a little curious about where words come from and what insight their earlier definitions offer. If you look at the Online Etymology Dictionary, you will discover the root word for "influence" translates roughly to the idea of "flowing in." At least that is the way it was thought of back in the thirteenth century. Granted, that was a long time ago, but it still has something important for you today when you think about the kind of influence you have, or hope to have, on others.

To help explore the merits of this idea, let's use something big, like the sun, as an example, given its significant influence on the process of giving and sustaining life. Think about how the sun works. Every day, you experience the sun's light and warmth *flowing in* to the world, to your world, and asking nothing in return. Its influence is felt when you don't see it—even on a cloudy day or dark night. And the sun is always there, even if you don't think about it. You might say that it quietly stands in its place, unconditionally delivering its gifts to all living things. It is ever influencing by giving in two familiar ways: through its way of "being" (light and energy) and by contributing through "doing" (radiating). Of course, all plants and trees gladly receive these gifts and use them to create a gift of their own—life-sustaining oxygen.

You can't help but notice how the sun's influence flowing in to the world is a natural expression of its unconditionally given gifts ("being" and "doing"). The sun is light and it does radiate energy. These are its natural ways of being and doing, just as you have amazing "being" and "doing" contributions to radiate to the world around you. However, you have one thing that the sun does not. You have intelligence. You are more, because you have the power to direct your influence and your way of "flowing in" to others and the world. You can be strategic about it, including choosing to whom you give what and why, as well as when and how you will direct your contributions. In other words, you have power—power to do great good and to leave others better just because you were part of their lives (see Figure 4.1).

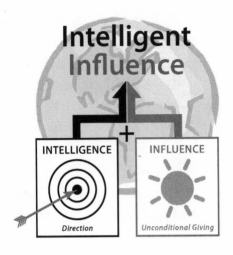

fig. 4.1

Here's the catch, though. Notice that you *can* be strategic. You *may* choose to give your gifts. Then again, you might not. You may never think about how your ways of "being" and "doing" could intentionally create a Shift Up! for you and others or how you unintentionally create a "bump-downer" experience that hurts. Because you have intelligence, it is also possible that you unknowingly try negotiating or posturing around your gifts, using them as a source of power to get what you want. This can also include withholding them as punishment or giving them as a reward. You can also end up protecting them by hiding them away, which is about the same as not having them to begin with. I guess this is the trouble with having intelligence, isn't it?

So this begs a question or two. Part of what makes intelligent influence *intelligent* is the way you choose to direct your gifts so they can flow into the world and make a difference. To this end, when you think about the kind of influence you hope to have, what does it look like? How are people better because you are part of their lives? How do you increase the positive flow in your relationships?

In thinking about your answers, there is one more influential lesson that can be drawn from Mother Nature about creating influence. It's possible that this one thing is the power source of this entire Strengths Strategy! But it can also be the hardest part of applying it. Are you ready for it?

Simply stated, Mother Nature gives unconditionally. Last I checked, there was no negotiating between the sun and the trees and the flowers about an exchange of gifts with each other or with us. The sun doesn't decide to stop radiating. The trees do not get upset and withhold their oxygen. These things are given without any strings attached, without posturing, protecting, or expectations surrounding them.

Can you imagine saying to the trees, "Sorry, I don't like the way you are producing oxygen right now. I'm not going to release my carbon dioxide to you." This seems ridiculous. And of course it is, but the equivalent of this happens in relationships every day. Never mind that the moment you fail to release your carbon dioxide, you die, just as you begin to die a little inside when you fail to release your potential gifts to others. If you try to protect them or set up expectations or negotiations around them, your energy and performance become depleted. You get stuck, and you can spiral downward endlessly.

Relationships die too, for the same reasons. And do you know why? They die because the life-giving flow stops. You rob yourself of the power of Strategic Interdependence if you get caught focusing only on yourself ("serve me"). This is the biggest enemy of your own ability to have powerful, lasting, and intelligent influence.

How to Intelligently Influence Others

Let's get wise here and see if we can't figure out how to strategically put intelligence and influence together in such a way as to increase the flow of energy and the performance of all relationships and tasks in your life. We're talking about the kind of influence that is as steady and dependable as the sun and brings light and warmth to your life and to the lives of everyone who is lucky enough to be a part of it. And who knows? Your life may even exude the kind of influence that feels as big and as far-reaching as the sun.

First, let's translate what we've been learning into a Strengths Strategy that you can apply. This means defining the Strengths Strategy of Intelligently Influencing Others in a way that is likely starting to sound a little familiar. You see, strategy is always about options and deciding which way you will go. In other words, you always have choices! Here are the two significant decisions that the Strengths Strategy of Intelligently Influencing Others points you toward:

1. The choice to direct the flow of your strengths to best serve the purposes and people that matter to you

2. The choice to allow your being/doing contributions to flow to others unconditionally (once you have determined the direction they will flow)

I'm including an overview of this process to help you convert your choices into action.

Choice #1: Direct the Flow of Your Strengths

When I refer to this first important decision, I am talking about your choice to seek and find ways to contribute and serve others by using your being/doing gifts. At this stage you are choosing to give your gifts to make a difference rather than not using them, using them only for yourself, or not choosing to even think about how your gifts might benefit others. To help you, remember it this way: "Choose to use." And to help you do this, these two questions can prompt you about where to look and how to have a positive impact: *What do I need? How can I serve here?*

Ironically, if you don't choose to use your gifts or think about how, when, or with whom you might use them, you have also made a choice (the choice not to choose). This means that you have chosen to select your "default setting," and the way your strengths show up will be entirely determined by others and by outside factors. This means you'll be stuck in reactivity, allowing your emotions and the emotions of others to be in the driver's seat. It means a lot of "bumper-downer" experiences where your strengths become flipped into weaknesses, which is exactly what often happens when you are not consciously choosing.

By the way, this reactivity is a great indicator that you have not activated your intelligence wisely.

Choice #2: Give Your Gifts Unconditionally

Your second choice in the Intelligently Influencing Others equation is to choose Strategic Interdependence as the mind-set from which you unconditionally give your gifts (including your ways of being and doing). Don't worry! We are not talking about the expectation that you give, give, give until you are entirely depleted. It also doesn't mean that you give whenever and wherever you can. The reason for this is that giving indiscriminately may not truly be in the service of others, as you disable people by doing too much for them. Finally, it also does not mean protecting, posturing, or negotiating the use of your gifts. After all:

▸ Protecting (hiding) your gifts is a function of Dependence and will throw you quickly into being The Victim.

▸ On the other hand, Independence and being The Hero come when you get caught posturing around (or withholding) your gifts as a reflection of your power.

▸ When you negotiate around your gifts, you put yourself squarely at Codependence and become trapped as The Player (in a relationship game that doesn't serve anyone).

▸ And when you choose to give your being/doing strengths unconditionally, you choose Strategic Interdependence.

To help you remember this, think "choose to lose." This is about choosing to put down, discard, and let go of anything that gets in your way of freely giving what you have and what you are. It's about saying no to "serve me" so you can say yes to "serve us/others." As I've heard my good friend Simon Bailey, a best-selling author and super-star speaker, say, "You have to let it go so you can let it come."

You can't freely give if you have flow blockers that are getting in your way. Two questions that can prompt you to make this choice when you need to are: "What is stopping me from fully giving?" "How will I let it go?"

> 66
> ### You have to let it go, so you can let it come.
> 99

Finding Flow

Each of the choices for this Strengths Strategy require intelligence, because they require that you make decisions about how you will wisely direct the giving of your strengths. Each choice also involves influence, including letting yourself "flow in" to others and the world from a place of Strategic Interdependence.

When you do this, you engage openly, without the interference of barriers or blockers. You need influence and intelligence, so you can be discerning about giving. Then you can give and live with your heart open. You can let go of any fear of failure or judgment or worry about not knowing enough, getting it wrong, or not having someone appreciate or like you. If this sounds like a challenging balancing act, you would be 100 percent right about that!

Yet it is possible. It is much easier once you become acquainted with the Flow Factors that help you to wisely and freely use your strengths to influence others positively. These Flow Factors are the most significant things you can choose to increase the likelihood of responding to others with intelligent influence. They will also help you to be wise when using your gifts. The Flow Factors are simple. Learning them will empower you to remove your own flow blockers so you can get in and stay in flow with yourself and others.

Before I introduce you to these factors and give you a chance to discern them for yourself, I want to share a story of a young man who was making wise use of his Flow Factors in an extremely challenging situation. In reading his story, think about what had to be present for him to demonstrate the kind of intelligent influence that he did.

At an addiction recovery center in Arizona, a staff member named Tom suddenly found himself with a large, angry resident who was on an emotional tirade. Choosing not to be sucked in by emotion or fearful of the resident's size or emotional instability, Tom calmly held his ground. With a quiet and gentle voice, he asked, "What is it that you are needing right now?" Tom's way of being was open and authentic, and he exuded genuine kindness.

The upset man studied Tom's face for a moment, cocked his head ever so slightly, and then, almost instantly, his eyes filled with tears, which spilled down his cheeks. His anger was gone as fast as it had come. Ashamed, he dropped his head, and his shoulders began to tremble. In that moment there was something almost childlike about him, in stark contrast to the threatening figure he presented a few moments earlier. The man was struggling to compose himself.

Tom stood waiting patiently and gave the resident all the time and space he needed. Tom's eyes were filled with compassion, yet he knew the importance of letting the man own what was happening.

Finally, wiping his eyes with the back of his hand, the resident looked up. All he said was, "I guess I just want someone who can understand how I feel." There was a pause, and Tom let his body language and his eyes respond for him. The man then added sadly, "I suppose I don't know how to say that very well or even how to ask for help."

With that, Tom just smiled at him for a moment and then replied, "How would you like us to respond to that? It sounds like you're someone who likes real conversation and a good heart-to-heart every so often."

Eyes now soft, the resident smiled back. "Well," he said, "the sunset is kind of nice tonight, isn't it? And the mesa is looking beautiful. You want to go sit down and watch it with me for a while?"

The two men then made their way out toward the red rock hills and sat there talking like two old friends until the stars came out.

Identifying Flow Factors

So, what did you notice about this story? What Flow Factors jumped out at you? When you study the events, what had to be present so Tom could respond with such intelligent influence?

To give you a little jump start, let me point out that Tom didn't leap right in and try to be The Hero. He wasn't The Victim either. The man's outburst did not intimidate him. Nor did he allow negative behavior to continue, meaning that he refused to be The Player. He was totally operating from a place of Strategic Interdependence. He was serving up both his "being" and "doing" contributions, and he was wise about how he delivered them. Clearly, the resident responded as much to his way of being as anything he said or did. Each of these things brought about a Shift Up! as Tom exercised intelligent influence.

This is particularly significant because you can see, even from that short snapshot, that the man was experiencing a bit of "pinball-machine" action, bouncing between the Dependence, Independence, and Codependence that we explored in Chapter 2. It seemed that he went lightning-fast from one to the other. He also was clearly in what is called the Toxic Triangle™, a frustrating, negative place, usually evidenced by blaming, criticizing, defensiveness, stonewalling, and/or contempt (see Figure 4.2).

Yet Tom neither judged him for it nor was drawn into playing the game with him. Why do you think that was?

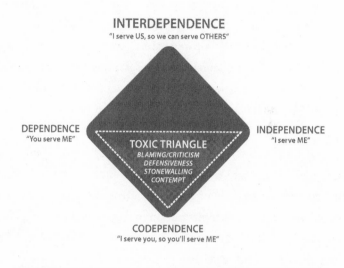

fig. 4.2

In considering your answer and studying Figure 4.2, think about how much time you, or others you know, spend in the Toxic Triangle. Maybe a person who came to mind is even someone you'd like to influence. In thinking about that person, notice how tricky it is to not let your discernment about what is real become judgment of yourself or the other. Judgment will block flow. As you can tell from our story, Tom did not judge the resident.

You might even say that Tom's own experience had taught him something, which made him quite wise beyond his years. He recognized that Dependence, Independence, and Codependence each have their gifts, and the only way you discover them is by being there and by having positive moments out of the Toxic Triangle to compare against. Tom knew that pinging around like a ball in a pinball machine was the surest way to discover how much he hated that feeling and longed for something better. He had already found that something better and used it well in the stressful situation.

It's kind of like he used his intelligence to first influence himself, taking whatever spark of goodness or potential learning he received from each of the three Toxic Triangle places and then blended them with the wisdom of his own experiences (see Table 4.1). This is similar to when the sun's energy combines with the carbon dioxide taken in by a tree to produce something new and life-giving (oxygen). Just like the synergy created between the sun and the tree, when you begin to intelligently combine elements together, you can turn even something you think is bad into something that's actually good. Tom's experience sure proved that.

Table 4.1 shows what it's like for you to do the same. You may even realize how your Toxic Triangle experiences can help you learn and discover the Flow Factors that will bring you to greater joy and optimal living. However, this will only work if you combine them and lean on them to guide you in your choices about where and how to serve others from a place of Strategic Interdependence.

Table 4.1

Toxic Triangle Origin	Potential Learning Gifts to Seek Here	Three Essential Flow Factors
Dependence	Knowing that you need to rely on others	Humble willingness to receive others' gifts and allow their "flowing in" to you
Independence	Self-responsibility as essential to growth	Confident contribution of your gifts and self-responsibility for your needs and frustration
Codependence	Agreements are important to togetherness	Intentional creation of conditions for optimal living, including designing relationships around contributions and needs

Table 4.1 offers a gentle reminder that no mistake, failure, or frustration is permanent (for you or others) if you learn from it and let it evolve into something that can help you to serve others better. No one is a throwaway because he spends time, or maybe even resides, in one or more of three places. The only difference between those who are trapped in the Toxic Triangle and those who are not is that those who are trapped don't realize where they are or why they feel the way they do. They also lack the knowledge to get out. And like the resident in our story, there also can be an absence of connection to someone who can

offer influence intelligently and inspire a different way of seeing and being.

Finally, you will notice the far-right column in Table 4.1 points you directly to the Flow Factors producing the biggest change for you and others. If you're going for big influence, that is a worthy place to direct your learning and to develop your gifts so you can help others find their own. Who can resist the influence of someone who is completely and utterly open to, and receptive of, others and their viewpoints and contributions? Who can resist the intelligent influence of someone who authentically and boldly offers up a wise contribution that fits the situation and another person's needs or someone who can't be riled or easily stressed? And finally, who can resist the influence of someone who makes the choice to intentionally create conditions for success (before problems surface)?

These are the factors that will accelerate your ability to intelligently influence others in ways that will bring great joy to you and to them. Now, let's turn our attention to the secret weapon that helps develop all three Flow Factors.

Confident Vulnerability: Your Secret Weapon

You may not realize it, but you already have access to a secret weapon with the power to increase your flow and your intelligent influence of others. You've experienced the uncertainty of Dependence, which gives you vulnerability. You've also known the sureness of Independence, which gives you confidence.

I want to offer a little disclaimer here, since the truth is that you likely flit back and forth between feeling confident and feeling vulnerable. Now you can see that all you must do is hold them together at the same time, and you'll have it—the secret weapon that touches every Flow Factor! If you can grow your Confident Vulnerability, you will grow your Strategic Interdependence and your ability to intelligently influence others.

> **"**
>
> ## You already have access to a secret weapon with the power to increase your flow and your intelligent influence of others.
>
> **"**

If you look closely at the first two factors, you will find the essence of the meaning of Confident Vulnerability. Spoken simply, it is this: *I know what I am. I know what I am not. And both are okay.* If you are willing to receive others' gifts, you are in a place of openness, receptivity, and vulnerability. Remember that vulnerability is the first Flow Factor. When you add to it the confident contribution of your gifts, you are displaying the confidence side of the equation. Putting them together is what Confident Vulnerability empowers you to do, as you draw the confidence needed from your strengths to help you to stay in the vulnerability of feeling weak or uncertain while being open to receiving from others. Of course, the third factor also requires Confident Vulnerability, as you disclose to others what they can count on you for and what you need to be at your best. In turn, this will create agreements and understanding that will increase flow in the relationship.

To help you learn where you are strong and where you are less strong, I'd like to introduce you to the Strengths Lens™.

Strengths Lens

As we explore the Strengths Lens (see Figure 4.3), I'd like you to consider the possibility that your strengths go way beyond merely informing what you do well and extend to shaping your worldview. Your strengths are constantly influencing your worldview. Like a contact lens that never leaves your eye, your strengths influence the way you see and experience everything, just like Tom used his own lens to navigate the tense situation with the resident wisely.

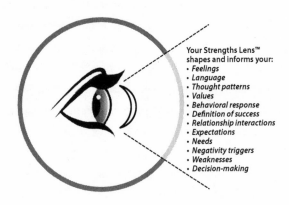

Your Strengths Lens™
shapes and informs your:
- *Feelings*
- *Language*
- *Thought patterns*
- *Values*
- *Behavioral response*
- *Definition of success*
- *Relationship interactions*
- *Expectations*
- *Needs*
- *Negativity triggers*
- *Weaknesses*
- *Decision-making*

fig. 4.3

Figure 4.3 illustrates how your Strengths Lens influences your feelings, language, thought patterns, values, and behavioral responses. It also influences your definition of success and, most especially, your interactions with yourself, others, and your work. Your Strengths Lens frames your "You should" and "I should" beliefs or expectations, which can trip your strengths into showing up as weaknesses faster than you can blink. You can also bet they inform the conditions where you flourish (the needs of your strengths) and whether you feel confident and vulnerable enough to deliver your amazing and intelligent influence.

To help you understand how this works, I'd like to invite you to think about a relationship challenge you are facing right now. Once you have it in your mind, take a good look at Figure 4.4 and imagine yourself as the person standing in the middle of the large circle. For our purposes, let's consider that this circle is the problem you are envisioning. I'd also like you to image 360 degrees of possible ways of thinking about or engaging with your situation, some of them being in the range of your direct or peripheral vision, while others increasingly fall outside of it.

Let's also assume that if you superimposed all the existing strengths around the edge of the circle, all possible ways of seeing or responding to your complex problem would be represented.

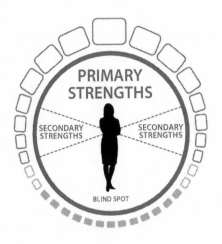

fig. 4.4

Notice also that it's impossible to experience all strengths to an equal degree. Some strengths obviously influence you much more than others, shaping your thoughts, feelings, behavior, and results. You can hardly see or understand other strengths at all. Your Primary Strengths are those directly in your line of sight. Your Secondary Strengths are in your peripheral vision, and your Blind Spot is directly behind you. Let's take a brief look at each of these to see what this means for you.

Primary Strengths

Your Primary Strengths have the most significant influence on how you see others and the situations you are in. These strengths significantly inform what you value, how you prioritize things, your operating beliefs, and how you define your purposes. They also inform how you define and approach work, relationships, failure, and your greatest contributions, as well as what you need to be at your best. They are also connected to your biggest weaknesses and can take you into negativity if you don't quite see how your strengths work.

For example, let's imagine that one of your strengths is being super organized. While this strength can be a great service to you and others, you can also find that you start to feel like a control freak the moment things seem to move beyond your ability to control them. You can then turn into a drill sergeant, giving orders to everyone around you to try to rectify the situation. This can leave you and others feeling weak, frustrated, overwhelmed, and drained. If you stop and think about it, you might notice why being in control and on top of things is so important: It's that the strength of organization is sitting right in the middle of your Primary Strengths Lens.

You should also know that your Primary Strengths are kind of like your mother tongue, the language you learned and have been developing since you were young. Strengths expert Alex Linley suggests you may have been born with some strengths in your DNA, while others were formed through your experiences. Either way, at this juncture in your life, you have come to think in terms of those strengths as your Primary Strengths Lens. You conjugate verbs and form sentences without even thinking twice about the feminine or masculine version of a word or whether the word means what you think it does. It's like second nature to you because you've spent so much time with it.

Secondary Strengths

Secondary Strengths are not quite the same as Primary Strengths; they are similar and tend to affect the same kinds of things, just to a slightly lesser degree. They are like a second language to you. Though they come somewhat easily, you may have to work a little harder to think fluently from them. These strengths are most likely prompted into action when you are with others who've developed them more than you. When you are around others who share these strengths, you find yourself using them more, so you are speaking the same language and connecting with them through your shared strengths.

Blind Spot

If Primary Strengths are the equivalent of your mother tongue and Secondary Strengths are like a second language, then your Blind Spot is a completely foreign language to you. Metaphorically speaking, you know a few words or phrases, enough to limp along but not enough to engage with confident fluency. Your ability to understand diminishes the deeper into your Blind Spot you go.

When situations trigger the need for these Blind Spot strengths and you are involved in conversations or interactions with people who are reflecting them, you can feel completely lost. It can be hard, or even impossible, to grasp what others are talking about or why the perspectives they hold even matter. You may not know how to connect with them, given how foreign they seem to be to you. You are so blind to them that you completely dismiss them or completely disregard their perspectives or behavior, in the same way you could shrug your shoulders and walk away from someone talking to you in an unfamiliar tongue.

Using Your Strengths Lens to Influence You

Think about your Strengths Lens and imagine what it could be like if you were to identify the six or eight strengths that you rely on most to help you serve others. Imagine that you knew exactly what the "doing" and "being" contributions were for each of your strengths so you could be intentional about where and how you used them to intelligently influence others. What would that be like for you? How would it help you? How would it influence your willingness to more freely give your gifts to others? Think about how it could also help you decide where to focus your contributions and which things to stop trying to do or be. Knowing your strengths can be a huge relief! It can give you permission to be the sun, if that's who you are. If you are to offer up your intelligent influence to others, you can't do it without authentically being who you are and doing what you do best to serve others.

Now imagine that you could also see your six or eight biggest weaknesses listed right there in your Blind Spot. How would it help you to know exactly what you can't do and which ways of being are challenging for you? What difference would that make in your confidence if you knew this? How would it help you with the vulnerability associated with receiving gifts from others?

If you think about it long enough, you'll notice how the Strengths Lens can help you make sense of the relationship melt-downs in your life. The Strengths Lens concept explains why you may have become frustrated with others, maybe because you expected them to be able to do what you can do. Your Strengths Lens, after all, suggests that whatever is easy for you is easy for everyone. When you realize that the people who make you the most crazy are those who show up in your life using strengths that are in your Blind Spot, you begin to see why you are not open to receiving them. You don't understand them or value what they are trying to give you.

To circle back to our story of Nolan and Elizabeth from the beginning of this chapter, you see that this is exactly what was happening in their relationship. This is why two amazing people who loved each other and were deeply committed to each other also began to feel like strangers in their marriage. When they began to understand the Strengths Lens and how it worked, and when they started to see what they each could do to contribute to their relationship and how their ways of being fit together like a hand in a glove, they could stop fighting and start loving again. It gave them permission to be Confidently Vulnerable. It gave them the permission and the wisdom to activate their intelligent influence to serve each other and the relationship in ways that were new and amazing.

I'll never forget our last session together, as they sat in my office snuggling on the couch like a couple of newlyweds. I would never have believed it, given the way we started. Something amazing happens when you start to see who you are in the bigger equation. Suddenly, when you own what you are and what you can be and do, it is easy to love the little bird that comes to nestle in your branches. You stop expecting someone you love to be a tree because you are. And you stop expecting them to offer the same "being" and "doing" gifts that you do. *That* is when you start to appreciate the song of the little bird in your life and how much it delights and soothes you—and how much you miss it when it's gone.

When this becomes your way of living, a flow of energy effortlessly happens, and with it arrives optimal performance and joyful living. When you are in flow, it is so easy to go. It is also easy to let others be in your life, flowing into you, which adds to your energy and deepens your ability to intelligently influence others and bless the world.

Note: If you'd like to explore your Strengths Lens further, go to www.peopleacuity.com to receive the People Acuity Insight Report™. This report will give you your "being" and "doing" contributions as well as your task-oriented and relationship-oriented needs. You will want to bring your Clifton Strengths-Finder results with you to get your report. Good luck bringing more of your "doing" and "being" gifts to the world!

Growth Zone Challenge: Power Points to See and Shift From

Welcome back to the **Growth Zone Challenge**. I invite you to think about where your breakthrough insights have come from in this chapter and how you will use them to further your growth. Study the list here and notice: *Which of the following was your biggest takeaway? What is one thing you will do differently to act on what you have learned? And with whom will you share your learning and commitment?*

- Influence is about letting your gifts unconditionally "flow in" to others and the world, radiating in perfect reflection of who you truly are, including your own ways of being and doing. Intelligent influence gives you the power to direct your flow to make a difference in ways that matter to you and others you care about.

- Three Flow Factors help you stay open to giving and receiving gifts intelligently. They are all magnified by Confident Vulnerability, which is about knowing what you are and what you're not and being okay with both.

- Your Strengths Lens shapes the way you see and think about everything, from tasks to relationships, from your feelings and words to your weaknesses and the way you make choices. Your Primary Strengths are your strongest strengths, and they are like a contact lens on your eye. Your Secondary Strengths Lens includes those strengths you can somewhat see and understand, but they work best with the support of others who have them. However, your Blind Spot reflects your areas of weakness. When others have strengths here, it makes you crazy because you just don't understand them.

Shift Up! and Feed the Need™

Your strengths reveal more than just the things you do well. They reflect the conditions under which you thrive. This one truth empowers you to flourish anywhere, because when you can meet the needs related to your strengths, outside factors lose their power to disrupt your flow or interfere with your ability to create potent positive impact.

—LISA GREGORY, MS, CPAC

Jason was just a regular guy. He loved football games under the stadium lights on a cool fall night. He loved cold pizza for breakfast and a good day of fishing with his buddies, complete with an ice-cold six-pack in the cooler. He had a reputation among his friends and family for being softhearted and willing to do just about anything to help others out. He was kind, funny, and easygoing—a real people person in every way.

Jason was also an engineer by trade and a good one at that. He was wicked smart and could go toe-to-toe with any of the other engineers in his office on the toughest projects and problems. However, he was also the guy who loved to hang out in the break room and tell jokes until others were laughing so hard they were practically squirting soda right out their noses. For Jason, that was a good day! These rare moments seemed to feed his soul. He loved collaboration and meeting with others, just to be with other people and to feel like he was part of something bigger. His prior job had plenty of all these things, but the new role in his company seemed to have less interaction among his colleagues.

It seemed that the longer he was in his role, the unhappier he became, sitting alone in his small, dark office all day, pounding away at his computer. That was his job, and that's what he got paid to do, like it or hate it. And he was becoming increasingly sad as he realized it was feeling more and more like he hated it. The reason he hated his position was that he had no idea how to navigate the unique people equation there and find an effective way to work with his team. This seemed to suck the life right out of him.

His team of engineers had a reputation for racing to their corner cubicles to tackle their to-do lists an hour before the other employees clocked in. Their extra-long hours seemed to be a badge of honor. To them, busyness was a sure sign that you were on the right side of the line and worthy of your paycheck. They were also private about their outside lives, and to Jason they seemed almost curt with one another. He couldn't figure them out. To him, they seemed distant and impersonal. It was almost as if they would do anything to avoid having to work together, engaging only to the degree absolutely necessary to get their work done. They seemed to pride themselves on not needing others and being able to figure out hard things by themselves without asking for help.

As you can imagine, Jason stuck out like a sore thumb among his peers. His energy, work ethic, and motivational factors could not have been more different from his teammates'. He had no need to compare how many emails a day he got with anyone or to brag about how early he got to work or how long he stayed after everyone had clocked out. The longer he stayed there, the less inclined he was to do either of these things, and his disengagement grew. Eventually he became the last guy to get there and the first one to leave. He'd also linger a bit longer than he should have in the break room, just hoping for a little interaction with someone, something to give him the spark he needed to make it through the day.

It didn't take long for others to begin to judge and criticize him, and he soon came to feel as though the other guys disliked him. He felt like the kid left out on the playground—all because he wouldn't play by their rules. It's not that Jason wasn't a good engineer, because he certainly had been throughout his work history, but the longer he stayed, the more he felt depleted, lonely, and frustrated.

Gradually his disengagement turned into full-blown depression, and he found himself drowning his sadness in a bottle almost as soon as he got home from work every day. Drinking became drunkenness, and repeated drunkenness turned him into an alcoholic. And Jason was not a good alcoholic. Eventually he hit bottom, and his wife took their three daughters and left him.

I met Jason about five years later. He was still in the job he disliked, but he was clinging to it like a security blanket, as though it gave him proof his life still had value. It was hard fighting his way back to sobriety after losing his family. The day I met him, I happened to be initiating a strengths-oriented performance improvement process with him and his entire team of engineers. This was the day Jason's whole life turned around.

We had just spent the morning exploring a rather unusual idea. It was the idea that if you could see and understand your strengths, they would tell you more about yourself than just what you were good at or what you loved to do. They would also help you see the conditions under which you could create repeat optimal performance and feel most alive and fulfilled. We had spoken of these conditions as the "needs" of your strengths. We also had been learning about how to identify these needs and to take responsibility for them so they could find joy and energy in their work, despite the conditions around them. Jason seemed to be paying especially close attention, almost as though his life depended on understanding the work.

That day I used the Clifton StrengthsFinder 2.0 to frame our learning activities. To help people see their uniqueness in relationship with that of other team members, we also explored Gallup's four domains of strengths, including: Strategic Thinking (high-level exploration/thinking strengths), Executing (get-it-done, work/goal-oriented strengths), Influencing (igniting and catalyzing strengths), and Relationship Building (connecting and people-building strengths). During this activity, we also explored the contributions and needs of each of the four domains so we could better understand one another.

Jason's biggest discovery seemed to be in seeing how different his strengths were from those of others on the team. He was the relationship connector in the office, the one who loved to talk about life, not just work, and he enjoyed seeing people smile with the sheer delight of being together. I couldn't help but to notice his demeanor change as it dawned on him that he was the only person on his entire team who was oriented toward relationship as the first and primary driver of work satisfaction. He was the only one who seemed to need others to look him in the eye or notice him in the hallways, to remember his birthday, to see him personally. In the early months of his new job, he gave his relationship gifts freely to others. But when they seemed not to be appreciated, he gradually withdrew them.

He'd always thought the problem was that the guys didn't like him and he wasn't good enough to belong. But in that moment, he realized he'd been thinking all wrong. It wasn't that they didn't like him, but it was true they were not like him, except in one way: Like him, they had been trying to give the gifts of their own strengths to everyone else on the team and thinking that everyone around them needed (and appreciated) the same things they did. They were hard workers who just needed someone to notice they were putting in fifteen hours more than they were supposed to every week. And instead of noticing or appreciating, Jason had judged this pattern as a one-upmanship game. They prided themselves on integrity and only wanted to give attention to their to-do list, feeling that activities outside of this were wrong and not worth their time. This, of course, is why they seemed curt and disinterested in "wasting" time. And speaking of time, they seemed to need a lot of it alone, as they were inclined to think deeply to make discoveries rather than talk through ideas the way he did. This made so much sense to Jason!

As he started to think more about their differences, he found his heart softening a little toward his colleagues, and he felt understanding and compassion rather than judgment. If their energy was all caught up in their own thoughts and the worry about deadlines and getting it right, there wasn't much left over for relationships. They might even have seen relationship building as a distraction. He began to see that he, as much as they, had built giant walls that kept them out and separated them. He also realized that the more he'd judged them for the way they were, the more he'd disliked them and stopped trying to understand them. He'd quit caring about what they needed or trying to offer help.

Beginning to process this, he realized this was the reason he'd stopped feeling alive. He had stopped trying to give to others— and what's more, he'd blamed them for this change in himself. The more he'd played this game, the more he'd shriveled inside. And the more his needs hadn't been met, the more his life had "shrunk," as though he were powerless to stop it. This was a lot for him to take in. When break time came and the whole room cleared out almost instantly, Jason just sat there with his head down, looking like someone had gut-punched him. When he finally looked back up and around, he and I were alone in the room.

"Can I show you something?" he asked quietly.

He pulled out a copy of his StrengthsFinder report. As I studied the report, I saw his strengths reflected his optimism and need for others' warmth, his sensitivity to others' feelings, and his need for their concern. Then he showed me how opposite they were to the top strengths in his department. The common team strengths revolved around such traits as order and organization, accomplishment, analysis, and gathering information. He stood there, as if he was expecting me to see the revelation going on in his head. I could feel the importance of this to him and how eager he was for me to see it, to see him, and to understand.

"I'm not like them," he finally said. "I'm completely different. Everything I'm good at, they don't understand." His eyes filled with tears as his story came tumbling out. He told me about his last decade there, his alcoholism, and how hard it had been to lose his family. He shared how it seemed like it had all started because these simple, misunderstood differences had built giant walls between him and his colleagues and had prompted him to start drinking because he didn't know how to fill the emptiness.

As he was about to walk away, he turned to share one last thing. With deep sadness in his eyes, which said more than the story he had just told me, he wistfully reflected, "If only I would have known this five years ago. I may have saved my family."

My heart ached as I watched him return to his seat, his shoulders hunched and his body language filled with regret. That was the moment I decided that every person in the world needed to understand how to Feed the Need of their own strengths. If it could prevent just one person from experiencing Jason's pain, then I wanted to make it my life's mission to help others know how to see their own needs and how to create their own conditions for joyful work and optimal living.

Feed the Need

While you think about Jason's story, let me offer you some questions to reflect on as you apply this to your own situation. First, when has something similar happened for you? In that situation when you were most frustrated, how did your strengths play a part? When you think of the most joyful and effective relationships of your life, how did your strengths work together to create these relationships? If you pause to think about them, these questions can help you gain insights relative to our exploration here. They can even help you see where and how you might find more optimal life and work experiences as you learn to apply this Strengths Strategy in your own life.

The Feed the Need strategy has two parts:

1. **Read Your Need.** This is about tuning into your own need by understanding the clues that help you recognize the presence of an unmet need and determine what the need is and where it springs from. You can't effectively resolve a need if you don't understand it.

2. **Lead Your Need.** This part of the strategy offers you places to look to discover strengths, tools, and resources that can help you take responsibility for meeting your own need so your energy can be fully available to "serve us" and "serve

others" rather than being caught in the urgency of meeting your need.

Using this Strengths Strategy is particularly empowering when you begin to realize, as Jason did, how much you are influenced by your own Strengths Lens and the way it can shape your view of yourself, others, and the situations you are in. If you are not careful, you may even discover how the needs of your strengths can dwarf your own contributions, to the point that you cannot use your strengths to bring you and others joy. Let's explore this further with an analogy.

Your Needs Can Eclipse Your Contributions

If you live in the United States, you might have been lucky enough in 2017 to witness a spectacular sight, something that has not happened in nearly a century: a total solar eclipse of the sun, capable of being seen from coast to coast. It was so exciting that it drew around 215 million people to watch it, which is almost twice the audience of the 2017 Super Bowl! It was an amazing phenomenon to behold, especially given that the sun, which is more than 400 times larger than the moon, can become completely obscured when the moon passes in front of it.

If you were one of the 215 million people who saw this, you would have witnessed the moon passing directly in front of the sun until it obliterated virtually all light, leaving darkness in its wake. Additionally, in some eclipses the temperature has been known to drop by as much as 28 degrees Fahrenheit as it becomes almost instantly dark. You may have also seen another unique pattern along with the eclipse, something called "shadow snakes." These are thin, wavy lines of dark, followed by light and then shadow, looking just like snakes slithering on the ground.

So, what does this have to do with you, besides just being a cool, rare scientific experience? You see, your strengths are like the sun, or the sun's influence, as we mentioned in Chapter 4. You have unique "doing" and "being" contributions, which set you apart from every other person, radiating out from you and creating remarkable influence. Based on the idea that you have about ten well-developed strengths, the mathematical probability that you would find someone who plays to the same top ten strengths in the same order is 1 in 476 trillion. So, in case you had any doubt, no one else is like you on this planet!

66

For every one of your strengths, you have a unique set of needs or conditions under which that strength will flourish. Your needs are as rare as your strengths, which is why you can't expect other people to simply guess what you need.

99

What is also true is that for every one of your strengths, you have a unique set of needs or conditions under which that strength will flourish. Your needs are as rare as your strengths, which is why you can't expect other people to simply guess what you need. The chances that your needs are the same as theirs is 1 in 476 trillion. And when your needs are not met, it is almost like they eclipse your contributions, as shown in Figure 5.1. When this happens, your contributions become darkened or invisible to others, and you can feel the energy drop like the temperature during an eclipse. You may even have your own version of shadow snakes—in the form of frustration, criticism of yourself or others, or judgment—that can make your skin crawl.

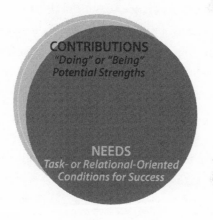

fig. 5.1

For you to shine continuously like the sun and fully bring your "doing" and "being" contributions (without your needs eclipsing them), you must know how to Read Your Needs. Then you must use your own strengths and resources to meet these needs so you can show up to intelligently influence others while discovering the joy of living and working in optimal ways. That's what this Strengths Strategy is all about.

Let's see if we can understand how it works by beginning with the first part of this Strengths Strategy, learning to Read Your Need.

Read Your Need

Your strengths sit on your eye like a contact lens, and you see everything through them, including how you serve others and what you need so you can accomplish this. In Figure 5.2, your strengths are shown as *potential* strengths and with good reason: If your needs are met, your potential strengths will shine like the sun, lifting you and others toward the high energy/performance experience of Strategic Interdependence. However, if your needs are not met, they will dominate the focus of your energy, and your strengths will be darkened, as though they were not there. Your strengths will turn into weaknesses in the absence of unmet needs and take you straight into the Toxic Triangle.

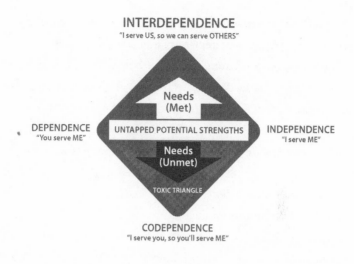

fig. 5.2

If you are like most people, you probably aren't even conscious of what happens when the needs of your strengths are not met and how you look to find ways to meet them. This is one reason you feel like you are pinging around in a pinball machine, caught up in "serve me" (trying to get your needs met) and hoping you can get back to high energy and performance. Have you ever noticed how you can go from Dependence to Independence to Codependence almost in a heartbeat? Unknowingly, you might be doing this to try to find the energy hit that comes when you are engaging your strengths effectively. Ironically, you will never find your energy until you find a way to get rid of the interference of your own unmet need.

Here's an unusual thought: Your Toxic Triangle behaviors

(the result of unmet needs) can actually be gifts to you. If you can see your frustration, depletion, judgment of others or yourself, and maybe your own unhealthy behaviors, this negativity can become your feedback mechanism. This is one way you have of seeing that the real problem is your unmet need and you are just trying to compensate for it. This seeing can help you take the first step to Read Your Need, which starts with simply recognizing that you have an unmet need in the first place, so you can notice your need and respond effectively.

The behaviors listed in Table 5.1 can prompt you to notice that you have an unmet need. Whenever you notice these behaviors showing up in your life, they are a signal that you have needs requiring your attention.

Once you have seen these or other negative behaviors as clues to your own unmet need, you can further the Read Your Need process by discovering what your unmet need is. This will help you find new ways to respond to it. Luckily for you, two clues can help you identify your need, including looking at your own desired contributions and the expectations you have of others. Let's examine them together here.

Contribution-Need Connection™

It is important for you to know that you have an unmet need so you can apply a Strengths Strategy to keep from getting sucked into depleting negativity. Let me offer you a simple, telling question to ask once you see an unmet need requiring your attention:

Table 5.1

Dependence	Independence	Codependence
Showing up as uncertain, hesitant, and anxious	Over-planning conversation details (thinking about what you will say, how you will say it before you are there)	Unwillingness to be authentic, including pretending that everything is okay (even when it is not)
Reading into someone's answers or behavior a personal message that says you are not enough	Not listening deeply, including preparing your next move while someone is speaking	Commiserating and gossiping, speaking negatively about others
Waiting for someone or something in the situation to tell you what to do or how to proceed	Judging the other person as less than you and being unwilling to trust	Excessively complimenting and validating others so they will like/trust you
Being reactive and impatient	Taking responsibility for others' growth; needing to be the hero and solve their problem	Unwillingness to explore issues or perspectives you don't understand
Looking for validation		
Judging others harshly for failing to meet your expectations or doing it wrong	Telling and expounding (expert mode)	Telling your story when someone else is needing you to just be there
Deflecting compliments or being self-deprecating	Feeling the need to be in control of what is happening	Agreeing with others, whether you do or not
Experiencing a lack of confidence in your own strengths or abilities	Being more inclined to talk, multitask, or think than really be with others	Withdrawal from the relationship if they don't live up to expectations or if they offend you

Given your frustration, what do you wish you could contribute to this person to help the situation or relationship improve?

As strange as this might seem to you, this question reflects a pattern that you probably experience all the time, without even knowing it. You saw it in Jason's story, both in his behavior and that of his teammates. It is called the Contribution-Need Connection. Simply put, this means you tend to give to others the exact thing you need. Remember how Jason did it? He needed to interact with others, so he made eye contact in the hallways, remembered birthdays, and hung around the break room, hoping to engage others and get them to laugh. He tried to contribute these things because these were also the kinds of things that he needed. When you are frustrated in a situation, if you pause to think about what you wish you could give to the other person or to the situation, your answers offer clues to what you need.

Needs and Expectations

If you are still stuck after asking this first question, look to this place to help you identify your need: Identify your "you should" expectations of others. When you are frustrated because others aren't listening to you, guess what you expect? For them to listen to you. And guess what you need? Right again! To listen to them.

This pattern reflects your Strengths Lens: When you are good at certain things, you also expect others to be able to do these same things as well. It also suggests how you want others to behave, given the unique needs connected to our strengths. Like a heat-seeking missile, you are unconsciously looking for that which will light up the energy of your strengths so they can be well-used and so you can make the difference you want to make. If you can't acquire the target, you unknowingly become trapped in a searching, toxic spiral leading around and around the Depletion Zone. Your unmet needs will take you there every time, feeling the experience of weakness and hating every minute of it!

The Feed the Need Strengths Strategy is one of many Strengths Strategies that can help you escape the Depletion Zone, along with the feelings of aloneness, frustration, and lack of fulfillment that seem to go along with being stuck there. This strategy can help you stop the downward spiral as you Shift Up! toward a more joyful and optimal way of being.

You know you have completed the first part of this Strengths Strategy, Read Your Need, once you have—

- Recognized the origin of your frustration as being inside of you (your own unmet need and desire to contribute) rather than someone else's failure

- Realized what your need is by examining your desired contribution or your expectations of others

This means you're ready for the second half of this Strengths Strategy! It's time to Lead Your Need and guide yourself through an exploration that can take you right out of your own Depletion Zone experience.

Lead Your Need

I love the idea of self-leadership. It's empowering to know that you can lead yourself anytime you don't like where you are. Knowing that you can learn to Read Your Need well enough to understand how to lead it is such a relief. This means you don't have to wait for someone else to figure it out. It means you are not a victim of your situation and that you can begin to make use of the tools, resources, and strengths you have to help yourself. It's important to note that this is not self-serving. It's more as though you are serving yourself as part of "us" and then responding so you can fully contribute again.

> **66**
>
> **You can't lift someone if you are not on higher ground. —Harold B. Lee**
>
> **99**

You don't have to be a genius to realize how hard it is to intelligently influence others from the Depletion Zone. It doesn't work that way! Remember: "You can't lift someone if you are not on higher ground." This means leading yourself to higher ground, using the same gifts and talents that you might use to intelligently influence others. When we talk about the idea of Lead Your Need, we are focusing on three potential strategies that you can use to Shift Up! These strategies include—

- Activating honesty and nonjudgment in your view of yourself. This includes becoming transparent enough with yourself to challenge your own negative view of yourself or others so you can access your own resources and Interdependence with others.

- Humbly asking for, and receiving, assistance from others. This includes making clear, kind requests (not demands or expectations) of others with an eye toward Strategic Interdependence.

- Consulting with yourself to access your own strengths and resources. This includes looking at your strengths as though they were a wise board of directors you might consult with and asking yourself what each could add to help you.

Let's briefly examine them here.

Activating Honesty and Nonjudgment in Your View of Yourself

To access your own resources or to kindly and humbly make requests from Strategic Interdependence is nearly impossible if you are caught in judgment or shame. If you are, you can realize that this is a universal human experience, almost as common as breathing. When you have dropped into the Depletion Zone, you are having an experience of weakness. When this happens, you feel weak. If you are like most people, you've been taught that this is bad, and you feel bad because you are feeling weak or have weaknesses.

You lie to yourself and others if you do not admit or recognize that this is simply a part of being human. Recognizing this happens to be the first step out of it. Your Confident Vulnerability can help you as you anchor in your strengths (what you are) so you can also be okay with what you are not. This honesty and transparency can help you see and use your own resources wisely to help you get out. Awareness of your strengths will also give you the courage to ask for help whenever you are stuck.

Humbly Asking for, and Receiving, Assistance from Others

If you and I were mountain climbing and you were having trouble getting over the last large divide to get to the top, chances are you would have no problem asking for a little help. There would be no shame in reaching out your hand to me and letting me pull you up so you could stand next to me and see the amazing view at the top. It can be just that easy when you are stuck in a different situation and recognize that your own resources won't quite get you where you need to be. You could say something like, "I feel stuck, and I could use some help. Would you be willing to let me tell you what I'm thinking so I can sort it out?" With that, you might even offer me an extra direction, like suggesting that I not respond because maybe, in that moment, your need is to talk it out, the way Jason needed to.

When you know what you need and you can simply make a request, you will find that most others are quite happy to serve you, especially if you've been specific about what you need, taking out the guesswork.

Consulting with Yourself

What would you tell me if I were to ask you, "Why do your strengths exist?" Over the last two decades of asking this question, I've heard two answers: First, some people say that strengths are there to be of service to other people. And this is true. However, the second answer is also true: Your strengths are tools to help you in your time of need so you can better serve others. For you, this can be as simple as stopping to pay attention to what each of your strengths might give to someone else if you offered them to someone who had the same challenge you face. You can even use this simple question to guide you: "How could you use your strengths to serve another person if she were as trapped or frustrated as you are?"

Relative to this question, imagine that one of your strengths is natural curiosity and the ability to ask good questions. In this case, you might think to yourself, "What questions can I ask here?" Or "What do I need to get curious about?" If you are an empathetic person and sense the needs of others and you hear what isn't being said, you can ask yourself, "How can I tune into my own needs here?" Or "What do I need to say to myself and hear?" It's crazy to think that you can give yourself the same compassionate, comforting empathy that you give others, but it's true! You can!

Your strengths have so much to offer you. They can be like a wise, diverse board of directors inside of you, since each of your strengths has something different to contribute. Each sees different things. Each has different, unique ways of being and doing that you can give to yourself. When you are stuck, you can ask yourself, "How can I use what I have and what I am to help me?"

Let's look at an example of someone who pays close attention to, and honors, the needs of her own strengths so she can serve others. Shauna Davis knows it's not selfish for her to thoughtfully and carefully tune into her own strengths. She has learned through repeated failures that to fail to notice her needs is a sure way to fail in her relationship and work experiences and to show up in ways that she does not feel good about.

To this end, she has designed a Strengths Strategy for herself that she engages in nearly every day. You might even think she is crazy as you learn more, but for her, the absence of this strategy leaves her caught in a toxic spiral all day long. This is true even when she is doing tasks she is relatively good at and she enjoys. Without the needs of a few of her most important strengths being met by this strategy, her energy drops and her frustration levels grow.

To be sure this doesn't happen, she makes a choice to meet her needs before the toxic challenges ever show up. Every morning at 4 a.m., even on the days when her body is not ready to be up, she is off to meet her own needs before she is drowning in the needs of everyone around her, including her seven children, her husband, and the hundreds of people in thirty-plus countries around the world whom she lovingly supports in her job each day. You see, she has a strength as a deep thinker, and she needs time to think, to be alone, and to be engulfed by pure stillness with time for processing and reflection. This is the only time she has when she knows she will not be interrupted.

Each morning for her begins with about ninety minutes of quiet contemplation. Part of it is spent reading and studying inspiring and inspired words. She thinks and listens beyond her ears. She hears her own inner voice. She pauses and often writes down her thoughts and impressions. Part of her time also includes enjoying the morning sunrise lighting up the quiet country roads near her home and the sound of birds greeting her as she runs, wonders, and ponders.

She has learned that for her to feel strong and to live and work in optimal ways, she must tune into her own needs and then create her own conditions for success. This awareness and practice creates conditions for her to create joyful relationships and fantastic results most of the time. Her family and those who work most closely with her would all tell you that she most definitely does!

Her story suggests that one of the most impactful Strengths Strategies is learning how to Feed the Need, which is nothing more than seeing how to create your own conditions for working and living from the Optimal Zone. It is about asking yourself—

- ▶ What do I need? What do I want to contribute? What am I expecting here?

- ▶ What resources do I have available to help me get there? Where do I need to be more transparent with myself or others? What specific requests can I make to help me? What can my strengths offer me?

Every day you feed your dog, your kids, your plants, and yourself. Learning to feed yourself was one of the earliest skills you learned to survive in this big, wide world.

But surviving is not going to get you to optimal living and working. It simply is not enough to find joy, fulfillment, and a life filled with great relationships and outstanding outcomes. Thriving is what you are striving for. To get there, you need to learn to feed yourself in a whole new way, to feed your need—and not just when you feel the emptiness of depletion. It's about thinking ahead and planning for your needs to be met strategically before you are starved of high energy and performance experiences.

Are you ready to try this Strengths Strategy on for size?

Growth Zone Challenge: Power Points to See and Shift From

Welcome back to the **Growth Zone Challenge**. I invite you to think about where your breakthrough insights have come from in this chapter and how you will use them to further your growth. Study the list here and notice: *Which of the following was your biggest takeaway? What is one thing you will do differently to act on what you have learned? And with whom will you share your learning and commitment?*

 ▸ Your strengths inform both your ability to contribute powerfully to others and the conditions under which you flourish. Your conditions are needs, and they are directly correlated to your strengths. If they are not met, they can eclipse your contributions so they do not have a chance to shine.

▸ You learn how to Read Your Need by paying attention to your feelings and behaviors. If you are frustrated and not experiencing high energy and performance, you likely have an unmet need. You can figure out what your unmet need is by looking at what you want to contribute and by getting curious about your expectations of others.

▸ You can see how to meet your need by examining your strengths and your own resources to help you identify how to respond to it yourself. You can also get transparent with yourself and others and make specific requests from a mindset of Strategic Interdependence.

Shift Up! through ICU
Acknowledgement

We are all mirrors to one another. We cannot easily see our own greatness, and we need one another to help us see the difference we make in each other's lives.

—STEVE JEFFS, TOP 50 GLOBAL LEADERSHIP COACH

Ali Hafed was a Persian farmer living near the beautiful white-sand river, the Indus, over a century ago. Ali's farm was renowned for its beauty and for the abundant harvest from his orchards, gardens, and fields. He worked hard every day and seemed content with working his land alongside his wife and children. All things considered, you might say that Ali was well enough off and living the good life, if you don't mind the idea of a man working hard at work worth doing and doing it with those he loved.

In the evenings, Ali was occasionally gifted by visits from good friends, including one enthusiastic friend who loved to travel and had seen much of the world. One night as the two of them enjoyed the warmth of Ali's fire, his friend told Ali all about his most recent travels, which had included his first-ever experience of seeing a diamond mine with his own eyes. Ali's friend spoke excitedly about the beauty of the raw diamonds and how you could see streaks of light passing through them. He told Ali what he had learned about how they were formed: at temperatures well over 2100 degrees Fahrenheit, where the tectonic plates where shifting and the pressure was maximally intense. Ali listened intently as he imagined the fires below the earth's crust creating such wonders and beauty. He learned that night all about their discovery, where they could be found, and how they could be recognized.

As the conversation was dying down like the embers of the fire, Ali's friend left him with one final thought, something that became planted deep inside Ali and awakened a longing he had never known before. He told Ali that if he had only one diamond, *just one*, he could place his children on thrones, and they could have anything money could buy. They would never want when the rains failed to come. They would never worry about whether or not they would have enough for their needs. This one stone would set them up for life.

This was a curious idea for Ali Hafed, who had never considered any other kind of life besides the one he was living, having spent most of his days working sunup to sundown in the fields and orchards near his home. He began to think about what it might be like as he moved into his later years, with money in his pockets and his children in a place of prestige and wealth.

The idea of not having to work twelve hours every day to earn his living started to appeal to him, and it grew the longer he considered it.

Ali thought about the conversation with his friend often. He began to visualize what this new future life could be like. He could almost see it in his mind! A bigger home with more room, maybe servants to care for his needs and those of his family. He thought about how nice it would be for his wife to have finer things than he had ever provided her. And the more he thought about it, the more discontent he became. His enthusiasm for his work began to wane, and he started noticing the things he disliked about the drudgery of his everyday life. It was so predictable and so hard. He realized he was getting tired of "hard." This made it easy for Ali to become increasingly obsessed with the idea of diamonds and how much easier and better his life would be if he had them.

His obsession led to a choice, which may not have seemed realistic from an outside perspective, given the many good things he did have going for him. But whatever good things he did have were obscured by his determination to go and look for the white-sand river where diamonds were supposedly found. He was determined to place his children on thrones and to retire someday rather than work his fingers to the bone, particularly as his body creaked and groaned the older he got.

With great determination, Ali sold his farm. His friends and family suggested that he was crazy to do it, but he was not to be dissuaded. With tears of sadness in his family's eyes, he turned from them to leave, entrusting them to the care of his neighbors.

141

Filled with anticipation, he began his journey to find the diamonds. Even his family's sadness about his leaving could not stop him.

He began his journey at the Mountains of the Moon, looking excitedly for the remote treasure. Then, as the months and years passed, he worked his way eventually toward and through Palestine as well. Finally, he made his way to Europe. He was always looking for the white-sand river that was supposed to be the marker of the treasure hidden deep below the earth. His searching continued while the money from the sale of his farm dwindled, little by little, with nothing to show for his sacrifice and efforts.

Finally, his money ran out. Discouraged at his failure to discover the diamonds, he stood between the Pillars of Hercules at the shores of the Mediterranean Sea in Barcelona, Spain. He thought about where he came from and where he was trying to go. He was filled with despair, and a spirit of utter defeat engulfed him. He did not want to return home and declare his failure, so he chose the easy way out. When a great tidal wave rolled in, he leapt into the sea, where he hopelessly and tragically drowned.

At this point, you could be wondering, "And what is the point of this tale?" It might even seem ridiculous and ludicrous that anyone would be so foolish. But our story is not quite over, since it does not end with Ali's death.

While Ali was off adventuring, the new owner of his farm continued to work the land, just as Ali had always done. He harvested the gardens, orchards, and fields, season in and season out, appreciating gifts of being a landowner and the chance to create such abundance for himself and others. He was simply grateful for his livelihood and the blessing of being a farmer and working beside his wife and children.

One particularly hot day many years after Ali had left, the farmer was leading his camel home after a long day of work. The sweat poured off his brow and left his clothing stuck to his skin. He was glad to pause at the small river in his backyard to cool off and to offer his camel a much-needed drink. As they stopped for a moment, his eyes followed the camel's head to the water, where he noticed a beautiful glint of light in the sand at the bottom of the shallow river's edge. He reached down and scooped up the most beautiful rock he had ever seen. A sliver of light seemed to shine clear through it. He admired it and held it up to the sunlight, turning it around and around, watching the light dance off the luminescent sliver of light. Without giving it too much thought, he simply decided to take it home and place it on his mantel, since it was too beautiful to return to the river.

One evening, many months later, there was a knock at his door. It was the traveling friend, who had once frequented Ali's home so often. The two men stood in the doorway of the small home, visiting, when suddenly the guest noticed the beautiful rock on the mantel across the room. With great animation he asked, "Has Ali Hafed returned?"

The owner of the farm replied that he had not and asked what made him wonder. The traveling man then pointed at the rock on the mantel and asked him where it had come from. He quickly strode across the room, took it down, and held it up to the light. Just as before, the light sparkled and danced through the sliver that ran down the center of the rock. A smile crept over the face of the friend. He joyfully said, "Do you know what this is?"

By now, you have no doubt guessed that the rock contained diamonds. According to Russell Conwell, who made this story famous enough to be included in the Top 100 Speeches in America, Ali Hafed's backyard became one of the largest diamond mines in the world. It was known as the Golconda.[2] Of course, this happened after he went looking for diamonds elsewhere.

Ironically, the Kohinoor and the Orlov, the crown jewels of England and Russia and the largest diamonds ever found on earth, came from that mine. Just one diamond, that is all Ali Hafed wanted so he could set his sons on thrones. Yet the diamonds, from what could have been his own mine, graced the heads of royalty. Such a poignant and puzzling irony!

This story always resonated with me because Ali's experience, in so many ways, is the sad human experience. I call it the Ali Hafed Syndrome. It is characterized by walking over your own "diamonds" without seeing them and looking beyond the mark for answers that are just below the surface of your own life, if you know where to look for them.

Although, if you are like most people, you don't. It is so difficult to see yourself accurately, relying only on your own perspective and view. This is where the Strengths Strategy of ICU Acknowledgement comes in. It's designed as a tool to help

---

2   Russell Conwell, *Acres of Diamonds* (Philadelphia: Temple University Press, 2002).

you and others see their "diamonds" with greater clarity. So let's take a closer look.

ICU Acknowledgement

The Strengths Strategy of ICU Acknowledgement stands for "I see you." It is about you looking beyond the outward behavior of others, without judgment, to see the qualities, strengths, and characteristics of those who come in and out of your life every day. In some ways, it is a mini celebration and appreciation of their positive influence, including the specific difference each person makes in your life and that of others. It can seem like a small, insignificant thing to name how someone's way of being influences you, but it is not small to the person receiving it. The truth is, this is the most effective Strengths Strategy you learn, as it can bring about a Shift Up! faster than any of the others.

This Strengths Strategy revolves around a simple idea: that the most powerful gift you could offer others is to see more clearly and value more fully their own unique strengths, qualities, and greatness. It comes with the assumption that the people around you likely don't have a complete grasp of the way they touch the world. Consequently, they don't see their own "diamonds," the value of them, or the possibilities that are right in front of them.

You know precisely what I'm talking about, as it is quite likely that you are caught in the feeling of your own smallness from time to time. Not that you are small, by the way! But you may not know how to step into the bigness of what is possible within you in some situations. It also comes with the assumption that you are not the only one to wonder if you have ever had a positive influence somehow in the lives of others and if your way of being matters or makes a difference. After all, it's human nature to long to make a difference. It's equally human to have no idea if you are making one or not.

This Strengths Strategy responds to this universal need and fills that void—the burning need to know not just if you matter but how you matter. It is about proactively creating "bumper-upper" experiences with others and doing so by design and on purpose. You best serve others when you help them see themselves, including their own resources and potential, as you provide a steady voice of encouragement. ICU Acknowledgement helps you do that when you are specific, authentic, and appreciative. Let's look at how your ICU Acknowledgement can serve others in significant ways.

ICU Acknowledgement: Serving Others

For just a moment, imagine that a colleague approached you after happening upon you in the break room as you were in the middle of a stressful conversation with another coworker. He could clearly see the conversation was not going in your favor, even though it seemed you were doing your best to remain calm and open while you navigated the situation. As your toxic coworker exited and you sat there holding the criticism you had just received, your trusted colleague quietly said to you, "I couldn't help but notice the humility you just displayed. While you could have shredded her to pieces, instead you just listened, heard her, and didn't let her ruffle you. Your example has inspired me to be more compassionate with others who judge me and not let it get to me. Thanks."

What would that have been like for you? How would his comments have affected the situation? How would you feel differently than you might have otherwise?

You likely would have appreciated his thoughtful comment. His words would have taken him less than thirty seconds to share, and it was a little thing to him, but it probably would not have been to you. He may have been able to negate the toxic feelings almost completely from the previous conversation by simply seeing you as he did.

Let's look at this from one more angle. If you're like most people, it shifts your energy to focus on the positive gifts in you, particularly when you realize that someone else saw them and noticed your gifts and how they made a difference. This validation can give you courage to stay in the saddle, to keep giving and trying and serving others, when you might have otherwise felt defeated. Acknowledgement of this kind also leaves you feeling valued. In some small way, you made a difference, and knowing that is enough of a difference to keep your spirits up, even after a "bumper-downer" encounter with a negative coworker. Who knows? Maybe that brief ICU Acknowledgement could even have been enough to help you look at your negative coworker with compassion and kindness and to see her in a positive light, regardless of her behavior, encouraging you to embrace the Strengths-Value Connection™ as shown in Figure 6.1.

See how to celebrate others' different capabilities and untapped potential, and their value.

4.

See and feel your value to a greater degree, and thus...

3.

See better how to add value, using your capabilities to make a difference, and you...

2.

As you see your capabilities (including strengths) and positive untapped potential with acuity, you...

1.

fig. 6.1

The Strengths-Value Connection is something you are constantly influencing in others, in the ways you respond to and engage with them. In other words, when you help others see their strengths, you also help them see and hold their intrinsic value. When you pause long enough to see others and take a moment to share the qualities you see along with the impact they have, you have become the catalyst for a positive chain reaction. Figure 6.1 illustrates that when you help others see their strengths, they're more likely to keep trying to contribute by using them. They also feel more valued and valuable, and they are more inclined to pass it on to others.

> 66
> ## When you help someone see their strengths, you also help them see and hold their intrinsic value.
> 99

ICU Acknowledgement can offer critical life-giving and life-sustaining strength to help others see their strengths and feel the difference they make while they are still learning to see it for themselves. It can be almost as life-giving and life-sustaining to them as the Intensive Care Unit (ICU) of the hospital was to our little daughter at times when it seemed her life was about to be snuffed out. A hospital's ICU is a place of attention and focused care, and, in a parallel way, ICU Acknowledgement can get others back up and going again when the Depletion Zone is sucking the life right out of them.

The Gift of ICU Acknowledgement to You

As wonderful as it is to gift others with this Strengths Strategy, the truth is that you are the one who will ultimately benefit the most. It's easy to think that the choice to reflect to others their gifts, kind of like being a mirror for them, is only about them. This is not true, however. The moment you begin to sincerely look at others with kind, appreciative eyes and to value their specific and amazing contributions, something happens to you. It can even be transformational. Let me offer just one small example.

Many years ago, our family was on vacation in West Yellowstone and having the time of our lives. This had been a long-awaited opportunity for us to be reunited with our oldest son and his wife, who lived 1,000 miles from us. We'd been planning this trip for months, everything from the camping, fishing, and canoeing to the trips to the local theater and the cowboy musical. We were so excited to be there! And while all the things we did were memorable, the most impactful moment of the week happened on our final day there.

It was a Sunday, and we chose to pause from our planned activities to attend church together in West Yellowstone, even though it was in an unfamiliar building with people we did not know. By the end of the service, however, I saw someone I knew and whom I certainly never expected to see while I was vacationing. As I looked across the aisle, I was astounded to see one of my most treasured mentors and heroes, Stephen R. Covey, the author of *The 7 Habits of Highly Effective People*. I had been teaching his three-day 7 Habits program for years by that time and had listened to him so much that I could imitate his inflection and body language almost perfectly when I told his stories. His impact on my life had been incredibly profound.

After the service, I immediately made my way to him. I had met and visited with him before, and I knew how rare and valuable such an encounter was. I also knew that our time together would be short, but I was clear about what I wanted to say to him. As he took my hand and looked at me kindly, I briefly offered an ICU Acknowledgement to him. I was eager to share with him how much my life had been blessed by the light that emanated from inside his heart and mind, by his insights, and by his warmth and authenticity. I shared that these gifts had provided a catalyst for me to get out of my own fear and to step into my own possibility of using my gifts to serve, just as he had. I'll never forget what happened next.

He did not say a word. In fact, it seemed he almost had no words to say. His eyes became instantly moist. His face was full of humility. He just put his arms around me and hugged me, as if he were my grandfather, kissed me gently on the cheek, and faded away like the sun at the end of a lovely day. I still feel that moment in every cell of my body. Its warmth lingers on, and I count it among my most cherished life experiences.

I share this with you to show how I set out to give him a gift. Yet I was the one who received the most. He taught me yet another truth that day, one of many lessons I have learned from him. He taught me that when you seek to find the best in others, the positive energy comes back to you, magnified many times over! You will always find what you are looking for.

Find-and-Seek

Speaking of finding and seeking, you might remember playing Hide-and-Seek as a child. You'd count to twenty while your friends hid. And then you'd go find them, because you were "it."

In our large family this game was a favorite pastime of ours when we were young, made even more enjoyable when a fun-loving parent joined in, which happened frequently. Great hiding spots were all over our half-acre lot, complete with its full orchard, chicken and rabbit enclosures, and robust garden. I especially loved being "It" and being the one to do the "seeking." That was my favorite part of the game.

Now, imagine that you are "It" every day. You wake up knowing that it's your job to do the seeking, to notice the positive qualities in others, and to let them know what you see and how it makes a difference. You watch for them. You start to tune your eye and ear differently to see others' greatness showing up, and before you know it, you see it everywhere!

> **Whatever you seek, you find. And when you seek the greatness in others, not only do you find it in them, you find your own as well!**

My guess is that this is not the only thing you start to see, however. The moment you lift your eyes, looking to see others in a positive light and calling out that greatness in them, you begin to see other things as well and experience new, remarkable results. This is not a huge surprise. Back in Chapter 1, we talked about how your chosen way of seeing influences how you feel, what you do, and what you get (see Figure 6.2).

When you see greatness in others and share it with them, you feel great. You experience a Shift Up! to higher energy and performance, and your step is just a little lighter. You "do" with greater confidence and courage and find that your results and relationships are just a little stronger and better. Likely, they are much better than those moments when you are walking through life with your eyes cast down, all worried about yourself and your problems, weaknesses, or failures that need your attention.

The bottom line is this: Whatever you seek, you find. And when you seek the greatness in others, not only do you find it in them, you find your own as well!

fig. 6.2

From Judgment to Unconditional Curiosity

This remarkable Strengths Strategy yields one final benefit in your own life. If you have ever hoped to someday find a magic formula for stopping your own negative feelings, frustration, or judgment of someone else, your waiting is over! ICU Acknowledgement has a remarkable ability to shift these things for you, at least for most situations and people. I didn't say it would be easy to do, but if you are willing to practice it, to challenge your own negative feelings and habits, you might be quite surprised at how much toxic emotion disappears from your life just by using ICU Acknowledgement. It can stop the downward spiral almost before it has a chance to start.

I remember when I decided it was worth a shot. My husband and I were raising three teenagers at the time, and I was watching the number of gray hairs increasing on my head daily. One day, Albert Einstein's definition of insanity came to mind as I was reflecting on a challenging situation with one of my sons. Einstein said that insanity was "doing the same thing over and over again and expecting a different result." It occurred to me that there had to be a better way of solving some of these challenges than the approach I had been taking.

I turned the situation completely upside down in my mind and started looking for my son's strengths, even if I could only see them in the smallest of ways or if they were showing up somewhat like weaknesses. I figured he was not exempt from the human tendency to overuse (or underuse) strengths when his needs weren't being met, and I shouldn't be surprised that it would result in an experience of weakness. I found myself wondering what might happen if I could see and appreciate his strengths and acknowledge the gift of them, trying to influence his thoughts and our experiences rather than judging and criticizing him. In our next conversation, that is precisely what I did when I attempted to identify the positive quality in him that I could see trying to show up. That became the focus, the springboard to our conversation, rather than starting with what he wasn't doing right. I was astounded at the difference it made!

He was immediately disarmed. All defensiveness was gone when he saw that I was trying to understand his intentions and what was behind his choices. It allowed us to have a conversation that deepened our connection and provided valuable learning for both of us. I didn't even have to lecture him. In the end, I think I learned more than he did, especially about the positive power to create a Shift Up! using ICU Acknowledgement.

What ICU Acknowledgement Is and Isn't

The win-win experience of ICU Acknowledgement cannot be understated! However, it takes some skill, practice, and real determination to choose to see and be different. It also means getting clear about what it is, what it isn't, and how to do it effectively. Let's switch gears a little and turn our attention to these things so you can better see how to bring this joyful Strengths Strategy to life.

Acknowledgement versus Compliments

To start, let's be perfectly clear about what ICU Acknowledgement is not. It is not merely a compliment, not that a compliment is a bad thing. A compliment focuses on the surface of what is happening. After all, "You look beautiful today" can bring a boost. But a sincere and thoughtful acknowledgement can transform the way you see yourself in a lasting way. Here is an analogy for you to consider as you think about how a compliment differs from an acknowledgement.

Imagine you overhear a conversation between a husband and wife having lunch, as they sit near you under a dining umbrella outside on a busy city street. You hear the husband say, "Holy smokes, look at that Bugatti! What do you think of that car, Honey?" The wife replies, "It looks like a slick race car, and I bet it can go fast! And silver is such a perfect color for it, isn't it? Kind of makes me think of a bullet." Almost to himself, he says, "Imagine having a car that makes 1,280 pound-feet of torque and can run up to 1,700 horsepower. Wow!"

In this exchange, the wife was looking at the surface. She saw it as slick, silver, and something that looked like a race car. She thought it was cool because it could go fast. She was admiring the outside of it and what it could do. While the husband was also appreciating that it could go fast and it looked nice, he was looking deeper and valuing what was beneath the hood. You could even say he was appreciating the *qualities* or *characteristics* that made it unique. He was valuing what the car was, not just what it could do. The surface view would be the equivalent of a compliment. Looking deeper and appreciating the qualities, strengths, or characteristics that underlie what you can see and how those qualities uniquely add value is what an acknowledgement is about.

You might be interested to know that Cheryl Walker, who coined the phrase "ICU Acknowledgement," offered her view of how complimenting, or recognizing others, is different from acknowledging them in a way that deeply affirms them. She suggested that often a compliment focuses more on what the person is doing. It recognizes their action. For example, a compliment could sound like "You did a great job taking notes in our meeting with Linda today. That was a lot to take in."

If you were the one receiving this, you might be glad someone noticed what you did. It may make you feel good to think that someone recognized you were trying to support or help in some way. It's not that compliments are bad. They just don't have the same Shift Up! power that an ICU Acknowledgement does. This is because a compliment only looks at the outside of you, what is seen and generally obvious. If someone offers you a compliment, it typically isn't focused on who you are as a human being or the way you positively impact others.

ICU Acknowledgement, on the other hand, is when someone really sees you. The other person looks beyond your behavior or actions or how you look or present to others. ICU Acknowledgement notices who you are, what makes you unique, and the way that uniqueness serves others. When someone focuses on your inner character, qualities, or way of being, he or she is meeting your deepest human longing, which is to be seen. This kind of insight from someone else communicates more to you about how others value you than any other thing someone might do. It also affects the giver, as that person loses him- or herself in that moment and creates a positive shift for everyone involved.

The next time you have the opportunity to create a double Shift Up! for you and someone else, you'll want to follow these very simple guidelines:

- **Identify the qualities, characteristics, strengths, or innate abilities** that seemed to help the other person to do what he or she did. For example, you could look for patience, dedication, commitment, perseverance, caring, thoughtfulness, creativity, initiative, enthusiasm, clear communication, or wisdom, among others. Here's how this part of the acknowledgement sounds: "I'm noticing how good you are at seeing how my idea will affect other projects, processes, and even other departments."

▸ **Honestly speak from the heart as you describe the impact.** Share how his or her quality or gift affects you and others. When the other person can feel your authenticity, it deepens the impact of your acknowledgement and creates a lasting effect. For example, "That helps me to see things that I don't see. I feel relieved to know that your way of seeing covers what I can't. It helps me see in a bigger, broader way."

▸ **Keep your acknowledgement simple and to the point.** A shorter statement, such as the template in Figure 6.3, delivers a greater impact and is memorable.

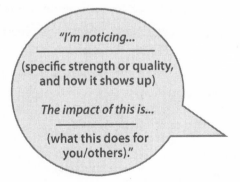

fig. 6.3

Here is an example of what this might sound like when you put the steps together in the template: "I noticed how patient you were with Laura today, how you were so nonjudgmental and curious with her. I also couldn't help but notice how much confidence it seemed to give her so she could feel comfortable enough to put all that information out there. You really made her feel safe. Actually, you made it safe for everyone. Thank you."

I'd love to invite you to take a close look at this example and to think about what you are learning here. At the same time, I'd love to invite you to think about the people in your life and which of them needs an ICU Acknowledgement from you today. What would you say to that person? What would the impact be if you were willing to offer it?

Bringing This Joyful Strengths Strategy to Life

Just looking at these questions brings back a burning memory, a sweet experience from many years ago. I had just asked these exact questions at the end of the first day of a two-day team retreat I was conducting, which ended with me teaching, and them practicing, ICU Acknowledgement. As the participants were practicing, I noticed that one of the women in the group seemed deeply affected each time someone shared an ICU Acknowledgement with her. She was more emotional than I would usually expect to see, and I was curious about what she was experiencing. This seemed to become amplified the moment I asked the two final questions about sharing an ICU Acknowledgement with someone specific and what the impact might be. It was as though the questions had burst open something inside of her.

After we wrapped up for the day, she approached me. She waited for everyone to leave and then quietly asked, "Can I tell you about something a little personal?" I had been working with her and her team for a few years, and we had developed a warm and comfortable relationship. I was touched that she would entrust something personal with me, particularly given her role as a prominent leader in her organization. She sat down across from me, and I gave her my full attention.

I could see that her feelings were deep and still near the surface as she spoke and shared how my questions at the end had seemed to prick her heart. She explained that this was why she felt so tender and emotions were bubbling up for her. Apparently when I had asked, "Who in your life needs an ICU Acknowledgement from you today?" she immediately had her answer, although it frightened her. What had come to her mind was how much an ICU Acknowledgement would mean to her estranged mother.

Her story came tumbling out. She explained that her parents were prominent in the small community nearby where she had grown up. They were well respected and admired for their traditional values, their work ethic, and the many ways they lifted and served others. As you might be able to imagine, they were not overwhelmingly enthusiastic when she, as a teenager, revealed to them that she was pregnant. Harsh words were spoken. Relationships were broken, and she walked away to raise her son, without their support and encouragement.

Her son had grown up without knowing and feeling the love of his grandparents, and bitterness had sunk into her heart. Though she missed them, she also had a lot of judgment and anger toward her seemingly unforgiving parents—not that she had been any better in that department, mind you. They had all allowed giant walls to grow between them, keeping them apart, and it had been almost twenty years. I could see why her feelings were so tender.

She told me how there was something that had happened as she heard others acknowledge her during our retreat. It melted her heart and left her feeling so valuable, so worthwhile. And it had nothing to do with anything she did. What moved her was that they saw who she was and that who she was had intrinsic value, despite her mistakes, weaknesses, or failures. As each acknowledgement came, this feeling seemed to sink more deeply into her, almost as if she were drawing from it light and connection that she had not felt for many years.

It gave her enough courage to begin thinking about what it could be like to take this new skill into the toughest relationship in her life. She told me that she was thinking about driving to her childhood home that night to see if a brief ICU Acknowledgement could break years of estrangement between her and her mother. I could see she was a little scared, but she was also hopeful. I sensed how much she missed her mother and how she longed for things to be healed between them. Her eyes clearly exposed her longing.

She turned from our conversation, resolving to act on her courage before she lost it. I heard her calling her husband on the way out the door and asking him to cover the bases at home that night so she could make a long-overdue stop at her parents' house. I could hardly wait to hear how things went.

The next morning, as I was setting up for the first activities of the day, she burst into the room. Her eyes were shining, and she looked five years younger, as though a burden had been lifted from her shoulders. She told me how all the way out to her childhood home she had been rehearsing what she wanted to say, trying to focus on the gifts her mother had so longed for her to see and which she had ignored for so long. She confessed this kept the butterflies out of her stomach, as she had no idea how she would be received.

Finally, she pulled into the driveway, and when she saw the lights on, she knew there was no turning back, however frightening this impulsive decision now seemed. Her voice trembled as she described what it was like to climb up the front steps and to ring the doorbell after being away for so long. She said she felt almost like a tiny girl standing there, waiting and wondering if they would love her or if they would slam the door in her face. I could almost feel her anxiety as she told the story.

With tears in her eyes, she reflected on the moment that her mother opened the door and saw her standing there. First, there was hesitation. And then the floodgates opened. She told me that before she even had time to say anything, her mother threw her arms around her and pulled her into an embrace that she would never forget, as the tears began to flow for them both. Shoulders shaking with emotion, her mother just hugged her and kept on hugging her, as though she never wanted to let go.

The two of them talked far into the night, having years of catching up to do. But she didn't look tired. Her face was radiating with joy. "I had no idea," she told me, "how she had been seeing what happened, or feeling about it." There was so much for them to share and learn about each other. And I was happy to hear how two hearts mended in unimaginable ways inspired by her desire to offer an ICU Acknowledgement.

I asked her what made her think of her mother when I had asked the question yesterday. She was quiet for a moment and thought about her answer. "Because I finally could," she told me. Being acknowledged by others had given her the ability to see in a completely different light the one person she had not been able to see positively—herself. It was a remarkable transformation. Among her last words to me, words that emblazoned themselves in my memory, were "It was like seeing her, really seeing her, for the first time."

"I see you." Such life-changing words. Such power in them and flowing from them, to unite hearts, to transform relationships, and to create an opportunity to begin again. You see, everyone just wants to be seen. The real question is, Who will do the seeing? Who will see the hearts of those who feel forgotten? Will you?

If your answer to that question is yes, then be prepared for your own tiny miracles. You, too, can be an everyday hero by simply seeing and acknowledging those around you, looking at others in ways that most people never think to do, and helping them see the "diamonds" in their own backyards. You never know the difference that may make.

Growth Zone Challenge: Power Points to See and Shift From

Welcome back to the **Growth Zone Challenge**. I invite you to think about where your breakthrough insights have come from in this chapter and how you will use them to further your growth. Study the list here and notice: *Which of the following was your biggest takeaway? What is one thing you will do differently to act on what you have learned? And with whom will you share your learning and commitment?*

- ICU Acknowledgement gifts others by helping them see strengths, qualities, and characteristics in themselves, which they may not see accurately or be aware of.

- This Strengths Strategy shifts judgment to appreciative, unconditional curiosity and helps to create connection, understanding, and more authentic communication with others.

- It simply requires that you name the quality or strength (way of being) of the other person and describe its impact on you or others.

Shift Up! through Creating Your Conditions™

When you become the creator of your own conditions for optimal living, nothing can stop you from becoming the person you were born to be or having the boundless impact you are capable of.

—LISA GREGORY, MS, CPAC

As a little girl, I remember watching the cartoon story of Hiawatha, the mighty Indian chief. I had no idea then what a remarkable legacy he left to his people and to the world. You may be interested to know that the English expression "bury the hatchet" has its roots in Hiawatha's story. It means something like "let it go," or put down your argument or your "weapons" that keep you from connecting and contributing to others. You might be interested in this little-known story that has everything to do with the Strengths Strategy we will explore in this chapter.

In the mid-1500s, there were two extraordinary Iroquois leaders, Deganawida and Hiawatha. You should know that the Iroquois people had quite a reputation for warring among themselves and the other tribes, almost as though they had an insatiable bloodthirst. This concerned these two great chiefs deeply. They loved their people enough that they were willing to challenge the status quo and try to bring an end to this pattern. The crying of widows and the sorrow of children without fathers or brothers rang in their ears and pulled at their heartstrings until enough was enough.

Boldly, the two of them decided to call the leaders of the Five Nations (the Mohawk, Oneida, Onondaga, Cayuga, and Seneca) to a council where they shared their concerns and their desire to find a way to live in peace. They were gentle but forthright in their call to cease all bloodshed among them and instead to form a confederacy. Surprisingly, the other leaders agreed, and a formal peace treaty was made among them.

This was a cause for momentous celebration, as it marked a life-changing shift for this group of people who had engaged in bloody battles for as long as any of them could remember. Women wept—this time for joy. And families rejoiced as they danced together and shared a great feast to mark the occasion. But Hiawatha wanted more than just this. He wanted them never to forget this choice so it could live on for generations in the hearts and lives of their children's children and beyond. And so he and his people did something so astonishing, so significant, that it could not be forgotten. It was an amazing act of incredible trust.

They chose to herald this new kind of victory by burying all their weapons of war under the roots of a white pine, deep in the earth. It became their solemn symbol of the peace accord and their new way of being. And it marked a grand new beginning of a new history for a people that came together around peace rather than war. It also helped them to remember and honor this change for many years to come.

Given the fact that they had been characterized by their infighting and military power, this part of the story is, in and of itself, quite remarkable. What is even more notable is what happened next. The legend suggests that in inexplicable ways, somehow the weapons just disappeared from the site. The oral tradition connected with this story tells of an underground river flowing beneath the tree that miraculously washed the weapons away so they could never be used again for bloodshed. So impactful was this story to the Iroquois that nearly a century later in 1644, the once war-mongering people were recorded by the Jesuits as boldly proclaiming to the people of Quebec their desire to "unite all the nations of the earth and to hurl the hatchet so far into the depths of the earth that it shall never again be seen in the future."

This remarkable story from the precolonial inhabitants of North America offers some interesting lessons for us to consider here. We can learn something from them about making purposeful, preemptive choices and agreements that can guide future decisions into paths of peace and joy. We can also learn from them how difficult it is to experience optimal living when you carry with you "weapons of war," including your own version of defensiveness and protectiveness from perceived ene-mies, both internal and external to you.

What if it was possible to reclaim an evolved version of this unusual ancient tradition, one that would allow for old "weap-ons" to be buried alive and new peace to replace them? What if you could create agreements with yourself about how to approach your own internal conflicts differently? It is impossible to effectively co-create peaceful conditions with others if you are warring with yourself. Peace flows from the inside out, as Hiawatha's story teaches us. He had "buried the hatchet" him-self, which is precisely why he could co-create new agreements with others, even those who had been his enemies. If this sounds desirable to you, you will be happy to know that you can achieve this by Creating Your Conditions.

Creating Your Conditions

In reflecting on Hiawatha's story, you will see another marvelous story that precedes this, the "story before the story," you might call it. This would be the tale of how Hiawatha was able to depart from the traditions of his people in his own heart and mind—to let go of the conflicts that had existed for generations and seek a more optimal way of living. No doubt this story would have its own miracles and marvels.

Hiawatha's experience, complete with his departure from old ways of thinking and his commitment to do and be differently, is what we are after in this Strengths Strategy. You are living your story right now as you discover how to proactively create your own conditions so you can live and work in more optimal ways. This may include for you, as it did for Hiawatha, which of your old habits to let go and what new habits to put in their place. As Henry Ford said, "If you do what you've always done, you'll get what you've always got."

> **66**
>
> ## If you do what you've always done, you'll get what you've always got.
>
> **99**

This strategy can help you break free from doing what you've always done, assuming you are excited about a process that can jump-start and sustain you on your journey toward the Optimal Zone. This strategy helps you see the conditions that are important for you so you can live and work in more optimal ways and help others do the same. The Strengths Strategy of Creating Your Conditions helps you clarify and make use of three important factors needed for you to be at your best:

1. **Seeing your possible contribution.** This includes identifying the contribution that you will bring to others to lift, serve, and make a difference. Focusing on giving your gifts in every situation, you automatically lift yourself and others toward the Optimal Zone.

2. **Exploring potential needs and barriers to being your best.** This includes removing the interference to

discovering your own needs and living out your deeper contribution. It is also about anticipating and responding to your needs in a way that will help you and others Shift Up! and stay in flow when you encounter frustration.

3. **Designing proactive agreements with yourself.** This includes making agreements with yourself, just as you would make agreements with others, to help you live from high energy and optimal performance. These agreements guide your contribution and the way you respond to yourself and others.

Let's begin to explore how this motivating strategy works so you can start to see what this might be like in your own life. As strange as this may sound, the first thing to know is how important it is for you to approach the Optimal Zone almost as though it were a destination. Think of it as a brand-new location that you are moving to, one that promises to give you a whole new take on life. It includes wonderful fringe benefits that compensate for the effort required to make the change. These benefits include things like finding relief from being constantly weighed down by negativity and frustration, and a significant decrease in Depletion Zone experiences that drain your energy and leave you feeling empty and disappointed. In their place, you will experience an increase in fulfillment, joy, purpose, connection, and aliveness. Does this sound worth the effort? Once you have just a small taste of this, you will easily agree that it is!

You should know this does not come without a price. You must work at it. Just like any major change, it will also involve some planning. Creating Your Conditions is your planning process, and you might be surprised at how it awakens your own awareness of yourself so you can see the best that's in you, the things you want to give to others, and what you need in order to deliver the contribution you desire to make. This planning experience helps you get from where you are to where you want to be and stretch toward the place of more optimal living and working every day. It can even be fun!

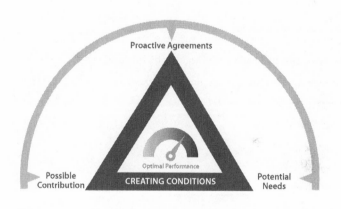

fig. 7.1

The Creating Your Conditions Compass shown in Figure 7.1 guides this process and helps you think about each of the three critical factors necessary for you to live and work in optimal ways. These factors are clarifying contributions, needs, and agreements. Taken together, these empower you to find new ways to respond to negative influences before they can drag you deep into the Toxic Triangle. At the same time, they also help you Shift Up! Let's explore these elements of this Strengths Strategy, beginning with clarifying your possible contribution.

Seeing Your Possible Contribution

The Optimal Zone is the destination we are pursuing. We should probably begin our journey by getting clear on what this zone is like for you and what your Optimal Zone experience is like. Allow me to pose a few questions here and see if you can't answer them in your own mind. The clearer the view of your destination, the easier it is to chart your path to it.

Think about a time when you experienced high energy and performance with others:

- ▸ What was it like for you?
- ▸ What were you doing?
- ▸ What made it a high-energy and high-performance experience for you?

Throughout this chapter, we will refer to this as your Optimal Zone example. Having a concrete example to draw from will help you think about the various elements in the planning process and how each relates to your experience of living and working in optimal ways. Let's use it now to identify some of the conditions that were present when you had this experience and which ones might be worthy of replicating in the future.

Give to Grow, Grow to Give

For our purposes, let me invite you to get your Optimal Zone example solidly in your mind so you can see it clearly. I'm going to make a small guess about your experience—that it probably involved your contributing in ways that you felt good about. I'd also bet that the way you showed up in that situation lifted others and yourself, and you probably felt like what you did made a difference. If this is true for you, then guess what? You've just validated by your own experience that high energy and performance are somehow related to contribution! This is a near-universal experience. The moment you focus on making a meaningful contribution of some kind, it creates a Shift Up! This doesn't mean that the contribution is easy to make or even that you feel perfectly confident about making it. Nonetheless, your willingness to offer up your gifts and talents is a condition you'll want to carry forward if you hope to create repeat Optimal Zone experiences.

I'm also going to make a small prediction about a second condition that was likely present. Check and see if this one was true for you. Did you find that part of what was happening was that you were stretching yourself just a little or maybe a lot? If you did, then you are like many others. When you are doing something that is just a little hard and you stay with it and let it stretch your knowledge, it gives you a rush. Was this your experience?

The truth is that if you are willing to hang in there even when you are uncertain and let yourself learn new and challenging behaviors, this can eventually move you toward the Optimal Zone, like a magnet. Sometimes, though, the process can be slow and halting. If you're like most people, when you are first faced with unknown or unfamiliar tasks, expectations, or goals, you spiral and swirl in your feelings of frustration, uncertainty, and maybe even inadequacy. It probably feels a bit like the Depletion Zone. But if you have a clear, desired contribution, some awareness of your needs, and agreements in place with yourself to think and do differently (Creating Your Conditions), this will help you to persist, learn, and stretch your skill set as you move through the Development Zone. Having clear agreements speeds up your ability to learn new things and contribute more deeply to your experience, ultimately exploding your energy and performance to an exciting and edgy place—even all the way to the Optimal Zone (see Figure 7.2)! When you think about it, you realize that growth matters if you are living optimally.

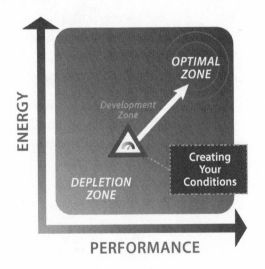

fig. 7.2

These two factors, contribution and the development of your knowledge (growth), were likely both present for you in your Optimal Zone example. This isn't a huge surprise, because they are related: These two factors inform and increase one another. They interact. When you give, you grow, and as you grow, you're more able to give. Contribution increases your knowledge, and gaining knowledge increases your ability to contribute. They are like multipliers in an ever-growing optimal living equation, as you will see in Figure 7.3. The more you know and the more you use what you know to benefit others, the more you expand yourself and create a Shift Up! for yourself and for others.

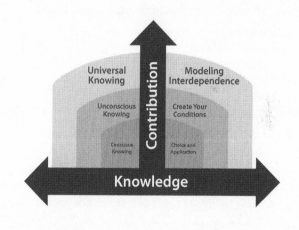

fig. 7.3

As you study Figure 7.3, you can't help but notice that you have access to knowledge that you are not aware of. That can be an exciting revelation, especially when the contribution you are trying to make exceeds your current knowledge and skill set. Just because you don't *consciously* know something, it doesn't mean that you don't have access to the resources and insight that come if you know where to look. And, of course, if you know how to create your conditions, you can experience greater knowledge and expanded contribution. You have three amazing sources from which you can draw insight and increase your ability to contribute. These sources, in so many ways, help you access your untapped potential and accelerate your way through the Development Zone so you can spend more time in the exhilarating Optimal Zone. As Figure 7.3 suggests, this includes Conscious Knowing as well as Unconscious and Universal Knowing. Let's briefly discuss each one so you can think about how this relates to you.

Conscious Knowing

Think about what you know that you are aware of, such as the facts, figures, places, people, and ideas that you have previously encountered and learned about. This is your Conscious Knowing. Your ability to grow the boundaries of your Conscious Knowing, along with the possible contribution you can make based on it, is equal to your choice to learn and to apply your knowledge. If you don't choose to learn or if you don't apply what you learn, you won't expand your contribution or your knowledge. What you don't use, you lose.

66

If you don't choose to learn or if you don't practically apply what you learn, you won't expand your contribution or your knowledge. What you don't use, you lose.

99

Unconscious Knowing

You might find this a bit harder to imagine. Unconscious Knowing implies that you have knowledge that you are not consciously aware of. One way to think about this is "instinct," which is what you do that sometimes feels like a sixth sense if you are tuned into it. You may not even know why or how you did it. You just somehow knew. This is Unconscious Knowing. Your ability to tap into this knowing comes in direct proportion to how well you create and honor the conditions you need to stay open and in flow. If you don't take the time for this, you can easily become stuck in reactivity and cut yourself off from connection to yourself and others. That is no fun.

Universal Knowing

Universal Knowing is simply amazing! It is ever-evolving, because it includes the knowledge, insight, and resources that are available around you and with and through others. It includes the synergy that comes from Strategic Interdependence, which further adds to the ever-widening body of knowledge and the ever-increasing circle of possibilities. You can't access this if you don't model Interdependence. The great thing is that when you do, you draw more people around you into living and operating from it. This just continues to add to the exponentially expanding potential.

Your Consistent Contribution

These three levels of knowledge are connected to your ever-widening possible contribution, which will increase over time as you apply this Strengths Strategy with diligence. They will also increase as you learn to live more from the Optimal Zone. This means getting clarity about the kind of contribution you can expect yourself to bring to any situation, even though your contributions tend to differ slightly from situation to situation and in response to the various people in your life.

You have a consistent, steady stream of contribution that you tend to bring to almost every situation and relationship in your life, even if you are not aware of it. You likely brought some version of it even as a child and are probably still offering it today. One important step in the Creating Your Conditions strategy is for you to identify what it is that you will choose to bring so you can be conscious and intentional about contributing it. The moment you withdraw your contribution, whatever it is, that is the moment your energy and performance start to dwindle. If you are committed to giving your gifts and you choose to focus on contributing, you are more likely to be able to stay at higher levels of energy and performance. This is even true when the situation starts to feel a bit bumpy. Isn't that exciting?!

It's important for you to know that it matters less that you perfectly identify your patterns of brilliant contribution. It's actually more important that you are committed to making your best effort to offer whatever you can give right now, however small it is. Your choice to reach out, to give, to lift—that is the difference-maker, the lever that lifts you up. When you embrace this, you can let go of waiting until you have found your perfect contribution and just begin. As Henry Wadsworth Longfellow said, "Give what you have. To someone it may be better than you dare think."

To identify your desired contribution, try this simple activity. Think of three or four times in your life when you made a difference in some way that you felt good about. For each experience, think about—

- What you did
- How you did it
- Your way of being as you did it
- The impact it had

What patterns or similarities do you notice? As you notice these patterns and become clearer about your contribution, you will find it is increasingly easier to claim your consistent contribution and create it in every situation and relationship you encounter.

Recognizing and Responding to Your Needs

If I were to ask you right now, "What do you need to be at your best?" what would you say? If you are like most people, this can feel like a tricky question and can be hard to answer. With a bit of prompting, I bet you could easily tell me all about the experiences when you were frustrated because of something someone said or did or that they didn't do (when you thought they should have). You could tell me about when you experienced excessive worry or anxiety about something or someone in your life. Whether you realize it or not, these are the moments when your needs weren't met. Frustration, and its close cousins, worry and fear, are the near-universal signals of your own unmet needs, as strange as that may sound.

In this part of the planning process, we are not going to focus on all the things you need or wish others would do so you can be at your best. Although it is good for you to realize what you expect from others and what you'd like others to do so you can feel strong and alive, if you make your energy and performance conditional on whether others will do what you think they should, you are going to spend a lot of time in the Depletion Zone. As you get increasingly better at living this strategy, you will find that the way you feel about other people is no longer dependent upon whether they understand and respond to your needs or not. You will be pleasantly surprised to find that the more you focus on being sensitive to your own needs and responding to them, the more accepting you become of others and the less you need them to meet your needs so you can feel okay about yourself or about them.

Do you know why this is true? It's true because the most important relationship you have with anyone is the one you have with yourself! Think of how frustrated you get when the people who are in your most intimate space seem insensitive to your needs. Remember how you feel when that happens? This can be crazy-making! Go back to the question about what you need in order to be at your best. How well can you answer that? The reason I am mentioning this again is that if you don't know your needs, it is difficult to be sensitive to them and to respond effectively.

> **The most important relationship you have with anyone is the one you have with yourself!**

This is the point of this important part of the planning process. Look at how you may get in your own way of seeing and meeting your needs and delivering the life-giving contribution that will lift you. You might get in your own way because you don't realize what your needs are or because you automatically expect others to know and respond to your needs. Sometimes it's the latter, but more than likely your bigger barriers to optimal living are not outside of you. They are inside you, and you have the power to remove them so you can deliver your contributions with greater effectiveness and see your needs more clearly.

This idea may seem a little foreign to you. You can find

yourself agreeing with it but not knowing how you get in your own way. This may include feeling a bit fuzzy about your needs or, even more importantly, feeling uncertain about how unmet needs could really interfere with optimal living. The truth is, it's hard to see these things. It's hard to see your needs and to track how they affect you and others. It can be especially tricky to find a way to plan for them, if you have not removed some of the blocks that get in the way of even seeing your own needs to begin with and understanding how they affect you. If this is true for you, let me share a real-life experience of discovering these things. You might also be interested to know that this Strengths Strategy was born from this experience.

Seasons of Change

Many years ago on a beautiful fall day in northern Minnesota, the trees were gorgeous, aflame with color, and the brilliant red, orange, and yellow leaves were still clinging to their branches. I was walking in the woods, as I often do, appreciating the beauty around me and considering how nature tutors us so well about life and how it works. In that moment, something dawned on me as I was admiring the leaves—something I'd not quite thought of before. It was a simple thing, but it started an important train of thought. It occurred to me how important it was for the leaves to come down, to sit beneath the winter snow, and to add their nutrients to the fertile soil so new life could grow. I couldn't help but notice the deep burgundy and green undergrowth and the black, rich soil at my feet and appreciate how important the falling down of the leaves was to it.

I then asked myself a question, one I had not considered before. It pushed me to the edge of my Conscious Knowing, inviting me to look deeper than I usually would have. I asked myself, "What do you need to let go of, and what needs to come down in your life so that new, richer life experiences might also come to you?" The answer seemed to explode up from an unconscious place, a much wiser place of inner knowing. I knew immediately the answer was right. I could feel it in every cell of my body. Yet I didn't know what to do with it. The answer simply was "Let go of your fear. Let it all go."

The more I thought about it, the more I realized this was my biggest need, as I could see how fear provided "inter-fear-ence" to my ability to step into the bigger contributions I could feel myself wanting to make. Fear threw barriers up and diverted my positive flow of energy away from what mattered to me. Its voice was like white noise in the back of my head, and it blocked me from seeing how to contribute with courage and confidence in the ways I knew I needed to. It also got in the way of my seeing what I needed to so I could give more of myself.

Fear, the universal "weapon of war," was alive and well in my life, although it didn't always feel like fear. I just didn't notice it a lot of the time. Often, it felt more like worry or anxiety about something. It would show up as stress, or sometimes it masked itself as frustration with myself, or even others. I hid behind it. I played small sometimes because of it. I blamed and criticized.

It trapped me far too often in the Depletion Zone, and I didn't like it. That day, it occurred to me that I could never get to a more optimal place as long as fear was my traveling companion.

I would say this was the day that Creating Your Conditions was born as a Strengths Strategy. It was the day I realized I had the power to stop this interference anytime I chose to exercise that power. And so I chose! Each day I began to set aside time to walk in the woods to "talk" with and "listen" to my own heart. I listened more deeply to the call of my own desired contribution fueling me, encouraging me to stretch into the "more" that was in me and to let go of the things that inhibited my growth. I chose to unconditionally hear my own "white noise," putting it on loudspeaker so I could begin to recognize how I interfered with seeing my needs. Then, little by little, I began to make decisions based on what I was learning and how I would respond differently when negative thoughts or feelings were triggered. These became agreements with myself.

This process tuned me into my own needs in more significant ways than I ever dreamed. I could now see them and plan to respond differently to them. And slowly I discovered more of my desired contribution as well. This process helped me see how to make peace with my inter-fear-ence and lay down my own weapons of war.

A year later, as another fall arrived, I was astounded to realize how much had changed. The fall before I had easily been living 75 percent of my life in the Depletion Zone, feeling almost constantly frustrated, stressed, and concerned about something. I was now living 75 percent or more of my life in the Optimal Zone.

My energy and health were better than ever before. I was getting more done and moving rapidly toward my goals. My relationships were the best they had ever been, and I felt fulfilled, alive, and excited every day of my life. And it had all started with seeing my needs, recognizing my barriers to my own contribution, and creating agreements about how to be differently with them.

Maybe something about this story could also work for you. It is as simple as asking yourself—

- ▸ What frustrates me?
- ▸ What things do I worry about the most?
- ▸ What beliefs do I have about myself or others as I look at those things?
- ▸ What am I afraid of?

The process of examining questions like these on a regular basis and listening to your answers without judgment helps you to become a good friend to yourself. With practice, you will become more aware of your needs so you can be sensitive to them and find new ways to use your resources to meet them and be free to give the best in you to others.

Creating Agreements for Optimal Performance

Agreements are everything. They are action activators in that they can jump-start you or provide staying power when you are doing difficult things that are important to optimal living. Agreements can also be action inhibitors and can stop you from doing things you'll later regret. For example, during that time I was walking in the woods, I made an agreement with myself that I would never again make my value equal to any scorecard. This was a hard thing for me, given that I have always been a high achiever. I decided I would not let my inability to accomplish something, my failure to get things perfect, or any other thing leave me feeling frustrated or inadequate. This stopped my negative thought patterns almost before they started whenever I fell short of the mark. It energized me to keep going on very difficult projects, even when I wasn't progressing the way I thought I should. This decision and agreement with myself gave me momentum when I needed it and stopped toxic patterns in their tracks.

This same principle applies when it comes to dealing with other people and to situations that threaten to draw you downward to the Depletion Zone. You don't have to go there, however. You can make agreements with yourself to guide your thoughts and your actions. These agreements will help you define who you are, your way of being, and the way you will show up when push comes to shove.

If you were to go back to your Optimal Zone experience, I'd bet that whether you realized it or not, you had some agreements about how you were going to work, either with yourself or others. They may not have been formal. And they likely were not openly discussed, but they were understood and more or less guided the way you worked and engaged with each other.

When you think about the fact that your relationship with others is framed after the relationship you have with yourself, you realize that having agreements can be the first step toward creating trust with yourself. You will also find that keeping them deepens that trust. It deepens your confidence as well, which gives you the power to be vulnerable. Each of these are prerequisites to living and working in the Optimal Zone.

Your agreements with yourself are all about helping you stay in flow. Your agreements keep your contribution activated and mitigate the negative effect of unmet needs. And while each person has unique strengths and contributions and equally unique needs, some agreements seem to apply to every single person, simply because they respond to universal needs. Let's take a closer look.

Be a No-Judgment Zone

Few things have more power to create Optimal Zone conditions than the agreement to operate from a No-Judgment Zone, as the moment you begin to judge yourself or someone else, you stop all flow. Energy immediately begins to nose-dive, and low performance will inevitably follow. The antidote to judgment is unconditional curiosity. The moment you let shame or criticism be replaced by a sincere desire to understand, to learn, to lift, and to help, you will Shift Up! and stay up while drawing others with you.

Bring Your Puzzle Piece and Invite Others to Bring Theirs

When you honor the contribution you identified earlier, along with stretching into additional contributions, you are bringing your puzzle piece. You are reflecting on your commitment to stay in a mind-set of "I serve us, so we can serve others," and staying clear about how you will serve as you engage in new situations with new people. When you also look around you for others who are strong in different ways from you and create room for them to also make a difference, you are inviting others to bring their puzzle piece.

Take Responsibility for Your Needs

In addition to your unique needs, and the Feed the Need strategy you already learned for responding to them, you might be interested to know of three universal needs that are critical to your ability to experience optimal living. Each of them invites a decision or agreement that will help you honor it. These universal needs are—

> ‣ **Being seen as unique.** When you see and value your own uniqueness, enough so that you can stand in it with confidence and vulnerability, you are honoring this need. To the degree that you can do this, you will find that others will also value your uniqueness. The more you value yourself, the more others will also. The potential agreement connected with this universal need is to choose to see yourself this way: "I am valuable no matter what I do or say or what anyone thinks or says. I cannot mess up my value. It is inherent. I know what I am. I know what I'm not. And both are okay."

▸ **Having permission to learn and grow**. When you give
yourself permission to not know and to have room to
grow into new learning and insight, new ways of being,
you honor this need. You can then let go of the need to
know everything and do everything all at once and just let
yourself evolve at your own pace and time. The agreement
connected with this is to choose unconditional curiosity
when you are frustrated because you don't know, don't
know how, or feel small or lacking in confidence due to
the feeling of blindness or uncertainty you have in that
moment. Some questions can help you: "I wonder what's
important about that? I wonder what the possibilities could
be? Who might have insight that I need? What past success
patterns will I find in my own life if I look for them?"

▸ **Feeling a sense of belonging and connection**. While
this need is typically associated with other people, you will
never feel connected with others if you don't feel connected to yourself. The agreement here is about recognizing your own negative self-talk, internal criticism, and
self-doubt and treating them like the weapons of war that
Hiawatha's people buried deep in the earth. If you are to
have peaceful connections with others, you must let go of
those "weapons" that interfere with a peaceful connection
to yourself.

As you look at these agreements, how many of them were
part of your Optimal Zone experience? Whether you spoke
them out loud or not isn't the point. If you were honoring them

and living without judgment, bringing your puzzle piece (and inviting others to bring theirs), holding yourself as unique, giving yourself permission to not know everything, and letting yourself belong, then you have validated the power of such agreements.

What would it take for you to carry them forward into your everyday life? What might happen if you did?

Beautiful Discovery

When you look at these simple agreements, you will notice they don't exactly frame the kind of peace accord that Hiawatha's people celebrated. But you will find they most definitely lead to peace. They lead you to a place of joyful fulfillment, as you spend more time operating from a place of high energy and performance. These agreements create a peace accord with yourself and a way to reduce the negativity in your life. More importantly, they increase your ability to bring your best to the world.

You may find that this entire Strengths Strategy and the process of Creating Your Conditions can become for you a Beautiful Discovery experience. This strategy helps you discover your own song or possibly add a new harmony to an existing song. It could also help you write a new verse or two, maybe even sounding something like this:

All of my life I've been searching for something
Something inside me to offer the world
I hear a whisper from my reflection
Calling my name soft and clear, this face in the mirror

Come step away, leave the shadow behind you
Come and declare what you know to be strong
Treasures are waiting for you to uncover
Soon you will see they've been there all along

Now is the time, time to let go
Unlock my heart, open the door
This is the song I've been waiting to sing
These are the strengths I have to bring
It's a
Beautiful Discovery
Beautiful symphony
So beautiful

Like a lonely child, I have been wandering
Focused on weakness, too empty to share
I've been a stranger to my life's purpose
So incomplete, so unaware
I've always known there was more to hold on to
More to believe in, more to become
The winter is fading, the seeds are awaking
Yearning for spring and the touch of the sun

Now is the time, time to let go
Unlock my heart, open the door
This is the song I've been waiting to sing
These are the strengths I have to bring

It's a
Beautiful Discovery
Beautiful harmony
So beautiful

I feel the strength, I'm learning how
I'm leaning in, I'm reaching out

Now is the time, time to let go
Unlock your heart, open the door
This is the song we've been waiting to sing
These are the strengths we have to bring
It's a
Beautiful Discovery
Beautiful symphony
So beautiful[3]

• • •

Here's to your own Beautiful Discovery! Here's to seeing your contributions with greater clarity and removing barriers that get in the way of your ability to see who you are and the amazing difference you make. Here's to seeing what you need better so you can courageously offer more of yourself to the world. Here's to the choice to apply this and other Strengths Strategies to your

---

3   This song is called "Beautiful Discovery." It was written by Cheryl Davidsen for DeAnna Murphy and for Strengths Strategy, Inc.

life so you can spend more time in joyful, fulfilling, optimal living—and help others do the same.

Finally, here's to the Beautiful Discovery of another verse of your own song, your own resonant melody, your own beautiful symphony sung or played with confidence and vulnerability. Now is the time for you to share it! It's your time to give. It's time to let go and time to reach out. It's time to be the best of who you are. The world is waiting for you, and it will be a Beautiful Discovery for them to realize the treasure of you.

So go and bring it. Gift yourself to others! Someone will be so glad that you did! Even more importantly, *you* will be glad, too.

Growth Zone Challenge: Power Points to See and Shift From

Welcome back to the **Growth Zone Challenge**. I invite you to think about where your breakthrough insights have come from in this chapter and how you will use them to further your growth. Study the list here and notice: *Which of the following was your biggest takeaway? What is one thing you will do differently to act on what you have learned? And with whom will you share your learning and commitment?*

- ▸ The Strengths Strategy of Creating Your Conditions involves getting clarity about your possible contributions, understanding your potential needs, and making proactive agreements to help you live in the Optimal Zone.

193

- Contribution and knowledge interact with one another and expand and widen one another. The more you gain knowledge, the more you increase your capacity to contribute. As you contribute, you learn and grow.

- The most important relationship in your life is the one you have with yourself. You create a relationship with yourself by listening to your own heart and mind, identifying your barriers to actively contributing in joyful ways (including fear, worry, anxiety, stress), and making choices about burying your own "weapons of war." This may be your biggest need, because it helps you to see other needs that interfere with contribution.

- Your agreements can include integrating the Strengths Strategies learned throughout this book. You may also want to make the choice to be in a No-Judgment Zone, to bring your puzzle piece and invite others to bring theirs, and to take responsibility for your needs. You may tune yourself to be particularly aware of the universal needs of being seen as unique, having permission to learn and grow, and feeling a sense of belonging and connection.

Afterword

Some might say that knowledge is power. Knowledge is not power until you do something with it. Knowledge, after all, without understanding and application, can decay and disappear. By itself, knowledge is nothing.

—DEANNA MURPHY, LISA GREGORY, STEVE JEFFS, PEOPLE ACUITY
THOUGHT LEADER TEAM

What a journey! You have learned how to see yourself and others through the lens of strengths and to let deficit-thinking disappear as you live from Strengths Strategies. You've discovered how to create Strategic Interdependence, to Leverage Success Patterns, and to Intelligently Influence Others. You've also likely found a little enlightenment in seeing how to Feed the Need, use ICU Acknowledgement, and Create Your Conditions to experience greater optimal living every day. You are now ready to apply what you've learned to be better prepared to serve others and the world around you.

Before we say goodbye, we'd love to offer a final story in the spirit of celebrating your strengths and your contribution to the world and how you can fully share them. This story is a bit of a parable of sorts, and who knows, maybe you will see some of yourself in it.

When our son Sean was still a young teenager living at home, his most cherished possession was his acoustic guitar. It was an exquisite handmade instrument that produced the richest tones and the most beautiful harmonics I have ever heard. It looked and sounded like a $5,000 guitar.

He played it so much that he wore the strings out. One day the A-string broke, much to his disappointment. He kept planning to replace the string, but homework, sports, his job, and other things demanded his attention, and he didn't have the time to stop and fix it. In its less-than-functional state, the beautiful instrument was mostly discarded and set in its case, out of sight and mostly out of mind. Even though the repair was minor, the guitar was, for all intents and purposes, unusable and somewhat "broken."

On a whim one evening a few weeks after the string broke, Sean went over and retrieved his cherished guitar, with its limited five-string capacity. He had missed the sound and comfort he felt in creating new songs on it. He picked it up and began to pick out a few notes.

At first he was frustrated that he could not produce the music on it as he had before. There was a gaping hole in the sound, and his perfectionist ear was not satisfied. But as he stayed longer and played more, he discovered something incredible.

The missing A-string provided an unexpected change. It allowed him to combine notes together that previously would not have worked. He found himself trying out chords he had never heard before and new chord progressions that did not exist on a six-string guitar. Little by little, he wove them together into a melody that was both haunting and tender.

Gradually, a beautiful new song grew out of the chord progressions. Its sound was awe-inspiring and captivating. Indeed, it was almost spellbinding. This song was a truly remarkable creation, and what made it even more so was that it never would have been discovered had the A-string not broken.

As Sean played the final note of his beautiful new song for us, a feeling of warmth and joy settled into the room, as it always does when energy and performance come together to create something that lifts and blesses others. His music always did that for our family. That was when the deeper meaning of the experience began to reveal itself.

As Sean and I talked long into the night, we realized that the beautiful handmade six-string guitar in its perfect state was something like a brand-new person born into the world. Somewhere along the way, if you are like most people, it is easy to begin to feel "broken" in some ways—by your mistakes, by loss, or through experiences that leave you feeling imperfect and less than worthwhile. You can even feel discarded. You may discard yourself, believing that you can never feel whole again.

Of course, that is just a story focused on your weaknesses and fueled by deficit-thinking. The story changes, however, when you begin to see your strengths and how amazing they are. It is kind of like discovering the beauty of your life played magnificently on five strings.

Allowing yourself to see differently, to have a change of mind about the value of your life, even though it has weakness and imperfection in it, allows you to begin to find a whole new song. Not *in spite of* your deficit, but *because* of it. You discover that you can make a different kind of music, which is amazing and beautiful, even though you come to realize you have some strengths missing from your life. Then you discover that five strings are perfect to create a melody from, one that inspires, uplifts, and strengthens you and those around you.

Everyone on the planet is perfectly imperfect. Yet your losses, your failures, and your dysfunctions do not prevent you from making beautiful music. Those things may help you create the most beautiful songs of all. The key is seeing yourself through the lens of strengths and effectively applying Strengths Strategies to create and bring your beautiful song to the world.

Set Your PACE™

To this end, Lisa, Steve, and I would like to invite you to set your PACE so you can increase your ability to create and maintain a Shift Up! in your own life. In the Foreword, you learned that PACE is a goal-setting system designed by 2014 Olympic silver medalist Noelle Pikus Pace and her team at Inspire Higher (for information see www.noellepikuspace.com). This system can help you create a simple plan for applying what you have learned here.

Because your strengths are situationally developed and trig-gered, we'd like to invite you to thoughtfully identify one or two situations in your life where you would like to experience a greater Shift Up! If you will, these situations can become your laboratory for practicing what you are learning so you can focus your attention on a handful of small behaviors and begin to apply them in a manner that is important to you.

You will find a series of questions here, including those derived from the PACE goal-setting methodology. If you will answer them, they can help you ensure that the knowledge you've gained transfers into your life and way of being.

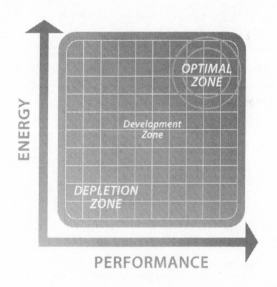

fig. A.1

Table A.1, shown here, will walk you through each of the PACE steps, along with a brief outline of what each step includes and some questions to guide your exploration. This process will work best if you have a notebook or a place to record your learning and growth so you can track your progress. To help you to see your own Shift Up!, you may want to consider asking yourself each day to rate your energy and performance (on a scale of 1–10) in the specific situation you are monitoring and to keep track of this in your notebook. This can help you plot your progress toward the Optimal Zone, as shown in Figure A.1.

Before you begin, take a moment to answer the following questions:

- **Situation:** What situation would you like to apply your learning to?

- **Strengths Strategies:** Which Strengths Strategies would you like to consider practicing in your situation?

Table A.1—Set Your PACE

PACE Steps	What This Step Entails	Questions to Guide You
Purpose	This is where you identify your bigger *why* and the motivation for your goal.	What is important to you about this situation? Why does it matter to you to create a change here?
Aim	At this step, you set your specific objective, including which Strengths Strategies you will practice, how you'll measure success, and when you will complete your goal.	What specific objective will you set? How will you measure it? When will you complete it?
Construct	Here you will identify what you will do first, second, and third and what will prompt you to complete the action. You will also determine when you will finish each step.	What precise steps or activities need to happen to accomplish the goal? When do you need to complete each goal?
Everyday Action and Account-ability	At this step, you will establish a daily routine and an accountability partner to talk regularly with about your learning. You will also identify accountability practices for yourself.	What step will you take each day to move forward, starting today? Whom will you share it with? How often will you visit with them? What other ways will you help yourself stay accountable?

Additional Resources

In the event you are looking for additional resources to help you Shift Up! and really stretch yourself into living and working in more optimal ways, you will be excited to discover some of the tools and learning found at www.peopleacuity.com, including—

- **People Acuity Insight Report:** This will help you understand what your strengths contribute ("doing" and "being") and what your strengths need (both task-oriented and relationship-oriented needs) to be at your best. It comes with a self-coaching guide.

- **People Acuity Accelerator Reports:** These will help you see the things that trigger your strengths into the Depletion Zone and trap you in toxicity. They will also show you how your strengths show up as weaknesses and the operating beliefs that can help you turn your negativity around. Each report comes with a self-coaching guide.

- **Online Learning:** You will find several learning modules that you can select and experience on your own and at your own pace. They are filled with games, videos, and interactive components that are sure to engage and delight you as well as deepen your learning.

- **Find a Coach:** Reach out to us to find a Certified Strengths Strategy or People Acuity Coach who might be perfect for you or your team.

- **Live Programs and Keynotes:** Our thought leader team and others on our faculty would be delighted to bring you live keynotes and/or full-day programs to help you experience the power of Strategic Interdependence in a highly interactive learning environment. This is a way to experience a living laboratory for practicing Strategic Interdependence, Strengths Strategies, and other People Acuity skills and tools.

▸ **Become a Certified People Acuity Specialist, Guide, Coach, or Facilitator:** If you are hungry to help others learn, you may wish to add professional certifications that will empower you to use the many tools and resources we have available to help others.

Whatever resources you choose, we hope you will find joy in using Strengths Strategies in your life. We look forward to joining you again in future books and learning experiences.

Here's to optimal living and to Strengths Strategies that will always help you create a Shift Up!

About the Authors

DeAnna Murphy, BS, MS, is the founder/CEO of Strengths Strategy® Inc. and its affiliate, People Acuity™, which has attracted over 300 partners in 33 countries. DeAnna is known for being a master at co-creating solutions to people problems and designing leading-edge transformational tools, content, strategies, and resources that are relevant to real-life challenges. She is also a highly sought-after coach, facilitator, and speaker and has presented internationally at multiple conferences, always delivering top-rated experiences.

Over the past twenty-two years of leadership consulting, DeAnna has developed a stalwart reputation for being a driver of engagement, productivity, and individual/team performance. Using both qualitative and quantitative research, and with an eye toward accountability for outcomes, she has seen her clients enjoy:

- A 259 percent increase in employee engagement

- A 90 percent increase in productivity

- A 475 percent increase in team connection measurement over a three-year period

- Three years of a 30 percent year-over-year increase in annual sales

DeAnna is an International Coach Federation member, with advanced degrees and certifications from Brigham Young University, the Coaches Training Institute, FranklinCovey, and the Gallup Organization. She lives in Minneapolis, Minnesota. Her family is the most important part of her life, and more than anything else, she loves spending time with her husband, children, grandchildren, and extended family.

Lisa Gregory, BS, MS, is a thought leader at People Acuity™ and leads the program development and delivery teams. With twenty-three years of business experience as an executive leader, trainer, coach, advisor, and successful entrepreneur, Lisa has extensive experience in learning and development at strategic and implementation levels. She has worked with leaders in 80 percent of the Fortune 500 and Global 1000 companies and has a deep knowledge of the challenges facing top executives, employees, and managers. Additionally, as an owner of multiple small businesses, Lisa has a deep appreciation for the challenges and opportunities of entrepreneurship. She has a passion for helping others bring their best to organizations, large or small, and to their own lives.

Steve Jeffs, BA, MPsych, DBA candidate, is a Top 50 Global Leadership Coach and organizational psychologist. Steve is part of the People Acuity™ thought leader, international business development, and analytics teams. Over the last twenty-five years, Steve has been involved in all aspects of leadership development—from executive to front-line leaders in multiple countries and companies. He is culturally dexterous, and he has attracted and led distinguished clients across the globe, integrating his broad experience with his doctoral-level knowledge. Steve is passionate about working with senior leaders and teams to empower innovation and ownership across organizations. As a scientist, Steve has ongoing research projects exploring the measurement of team climate and describing the complexities of shared leadership.